Inspirational Habits of the Wealthy

The secret behaviours that distinguish the rich and successful from the masses

(and how to adopt them forever)

Dan Keller

Contents

Download Your Wealthy Habits Cheatsheet

To accompany this book, I have created a printable Cheatsheet to save you time writing in chapter one. It is not essential, you can use plain paper, though printing out the sheet will save you time (and looks cool). The cheatsheet includes a Time Management Scorecard and a checklist to help you implement your new positive habits.

Grab your "Wealthy Habits Cheatsheet" at juicypublishing.net/habits

Your Free Gift

As a way of saying thanks for your purchase, I've also put together your free gift to download now online:

1. A relaxing **background track** to help you enjoy your reading time.
2. Fifteen beautiful desktop wallpapers with inspiring quotes for your daily dose of motivation.

Grab your Wealthy Habits free gift at juicypublishing.net/habits

Introduction

"Change might not be fast, and it isn't always easy. But with time and effort, almost any habit can be reshaped."
Charles Duhigg

Imagine lying on your death bed, and instead of family members surrounding you comforting you as you cross over to the other side, your dreams confront you. They begin to speak, asking, "Why didn't you give us life, we have existed inside your head for decades excited and waiting for the day that we would make an impact on the world. But now, we must go to the grave with you."

What a terrible day that would be, instead of dying empty, you leave this earth full, pregnant with the destiny that you failed to birth.

World-renowned public speaker Les Brown made this statement. He then went on to ask his audience where the wealthiest place in the world was. Some said Switzerland, others the United States, Iceland, Australia...Mr. Brown stunned his audience into silence and responded with, "It's the graveyard." Because there you will find businesses that were never established, books that were never written, inventions that were never created, songs that were never sung. Buried in a graveyard are millions of dreams.

Now I would like to ask you a question, imagine that you are on your death bed and your family is planning your funeral. What is your legacy? What impact have you made on the world? And what would those who you have left behind have to say about you?

Take two minutes to think about this before you continue reading.

Tomorrow is not promised, there is no guarantee that you are going to have another five, ten, or fifteen years to get it right. And when you spend time evaluating your life thus far and realise that if you left this earth today, you would be going with unfulfilled potential buried in your soul, it's mortifying. I want to ask you another question. If you carry on in the direction you are heading, what would your life look like in 10 years? Will you achieve your goals?

For many, the answer is "no" because you spent your life existing, surviving, and living for today. Afraid to break barriers and do something extraordinary just in case it didn't work out. You got comfortable and convinced yourself that success was only for a particular type of person, and that person wasn't you.

I believe you have picked up this book because you want more out of life, and I want to encourage you today that it is possible. You can have everything you have ever dreamed of and more, and in this book, I am going to show you exactly how to do so.

There is a formula to success, universal laws, and principles that, when implemented, produce positive results. If you study the stories of inspirational leaders, CEOs, entrepreneurs, self-made millionaires and other highly successful people, you will learn that they have several things in common, habits, and routines that lead to their desired outcomes. Success is not an accident; it is a very strategic and calculated process that requires extreme discipline and determination.

We all have 24 hours in a day, but what we choose to do with that time will determine our level of success. The rich understand that time is a valuable commodity, and once it is gone, you can't get it back. Therefore, they ensure that their time is spent doing the thing that will lead to their end goal, and they don't compromise with this.

Multibillionaire entrepreneur Richard Branson stated in an interview that he refuses to waste time on anything that doesn't line up with his vision. The average person claims that they want to be successful, but when you pay attention to how they spend their time, it tells a different story.

Since childhood, I have been an avid reader, I knew what I wanted out of life, and I was going to do what was necessary to get there. So, I made it my goal to read any book that would assist me in getting to my final destination. Within a few short years, I had built a small arsenal of self-help and personal development books, all of which gave me insight into the mindset and habits of high achievers.

I put what I was reading into practice, broke out of the rat race, quit my 9-5 desk job in UK banking, and my family and I now live an abundant life that has exceeded my wildest expectations. Everything that I have achieved in life came through applying the habits documented in this book.

It took me years of trial and error to figure it out, I read hundreds of books, and there were many bumps in the road, but I can now say with confidence that I am living the life of my dreams. Through this book, I want to help you do the same; if your bad habits have led you to a place where you don't want to be, it only makes logical sense that good habits will lead you into a place where you do want to be. I want to teach you how to overcome your bad habits and replace them with the good habits of wealth-generating highly successful people.

You will learn there is a distinctive difference between the thought patterns and behaviours of those who achieve their dreams and those who have conformed to the life that society has taught us to accept. Get an education and get a J.O.B (just over broke), retire at 65, and that is when you can start living your life on a measly pension that's just enough to pay your bills!

In the first few chapters of this book, you will find a whole new appreciation for the concept of time. If you applied the same energy that you put in your 9-5 into working towards your goals, you would have a completely different outcome.

You know what your weak areas are; therefore, each chapter focuses on specific habits that you can apply to your life to achieve your desired results.

The final chapter holds the key to unlock your true potential. It teaches you how to ensure that the habits you have learned become a part of your identity so that your subconscious mind is continuously driving you towards success.

The habits that you are about to learn are not new, they have existed since the beginning of time, and millions of high achievers around the globe have used them to reach their highest potential.

If you want to become more disciplined, productive, and resourceful in life, this book will allow you to tap into a reservoir of knowledge that has propelled the most successful people who have ever lived into greatness.

It is your responsibility to use your time in the most productive way possible. Time management is the first step towards taking control of your life and your finances. Once you learn how to use your time wisely, you will maximise your potential and start turning your dreams into a reality.

Are you happy with the life you are currently living? Are there things you want to do, places you want to go but you can't because you don't have the resources? Take a few minutes to imagine what it would be like to have everything you ever dreamed of, to be truly content with life, to have your children look at you with a sense of pride because they are free from the burden of lack?

What does that feel like?

The most powerful feeling in the world is knowing that you are in control of your destiny; you hold the pen to write the story of your life. Everything you have just visualised is possible if you are willing to put in the work. Don't allow another day to pass you by without knowing that you have put every effort into achieving your dreams. There is no time like the present, start reading and applying the life-transforming strategies in the Inspirational Habits of the Wealthy and experience guaranteed extraordinary results.

1. The Success Basics You Need to Know About

According to the Credit Suisse report, 1% of the population own half of the world's wealth. If you were to ask the average person why this is the case, the assumption is that anyone who has achieved extraordinary success has done so because they were born into privileged circumstances, or they are fortunate. The reality is that success is not a destination or goal; it is a mindset, and if you can change the way you think, anybody can achieve success. The opposite of the success mindset is a scarcity mindset, this is where wealth and prosperity are viewed as a limited resource, and there's only so much that can go around. You could compare it to a pie, where if somebody takes too big of a slice, there won't be enough for anybody else. With this mindset, people like Bill Gates are considered selfish despite the amount of money he has donated to charity, and the people he has helped that are less fortunate than himself. He is viewed as selfish because he took too big of a slice and didn't leave enough for everybody else.

Every successful person that I know has faced the same, and if not tougher challenges than everybody else. If there's one thing I've learned over the years, it's that greatness is birthed out of adversity. And when you analyse the habits and behaviours of successful people in the world, you will find that they all follow a similar pattern.

How do we Define Success?

There is no definitive answer to this question; like most, I grew up believing that the hallmarks of success were money and power, this framed my definition for many years, but this has changed, I have matured. You see, we all have our own ideas of success, what drives one entrepreneur may be the complete opposite to what drives another; and understanding how others define success, can help you with your definition:

Richard Branson: Even though Sir Richard Branson, the founder of the Virgin Group, is worth $4.1 billion, Branson believes that success is about personal fulfilment. In a post he wrote on LinkedIn, he stated, *"We have been conditioned to believe that success is about how much money you have. I don't believe this to be true because plenty of people have got money, but they are not happy. to me, success is measured by how happy you are."*

Ariana Huffington: *"Most believe that success is related to money and power; this is only partly true because there are things that money cannot buy. We also need to add wisdom, well-being and giving to this equation."* In her book 'Thrive', she writes that these factors combined contribute to your psychological well-being, and this is what Huffington believes makes you truly successful.

Mark Cuban: Despite the level of success he has achieved, his definition of success is relatively simple; *"Happiness is being able to wake up in the morning with a smile on your face, and I had achieved this when I was poor living in a 3-bedroom apartment with three guys sleeping on the floor."* So, to Cuban success isn't about what you own; it's about being happy regardless of your circumstances.

Maya Angelou: Maya Angelou is no longer with us, but she left a legacy in her books that will never be erased. To the great poet, success meant, *"Liking yourself, liking what you do, and liking how you do it."*

Bill Gates: With a net worth of over $100 billion, Bill Gates is the second wealthiest person in the world after Amazon's Jeff Bezos. But to him, success is not about money or power; it is about building strong relationships and leaving a legacy that will make you proud.

Warren Buffett: To Mr Buffet, success is defined by whether the people around you feel loved and happy and how much they love you because of the way you have affected their life. He believes that success is about making an impact on the world, raising well-rounded children, and helping people who are in need.

How do we Measure Success?

Job title, happiness, and wealth are some of the most common indicators of success. Success must be measured in the right way because this will determine how you spend your effort and your time. If success is not measured according to what you view as important, it will be challenging to work towards achieving your goals.

What are your values? Extremely motivated people spend a lot of their time on the execution instead of focusing on metrics. It takes hard work to achieve success but knowing which metrics to achieve is essential. At this moment, I want you to get a pen and paper, and write down everything you value, ignore what everyone else has told you and write from the heart. Forget the fact that your parents wanted you to be a doctor, lawyer, or accountant. If you feel that your values conflict with what you were raised with, it's time to establish your own set of values. Once you do this, it will become easier for you to measure success.

While walking in the direction of your metrics for success, don't allow anyone to make you feel like a failure because you refuse to conform to somebody else's standards. Your friend Justin might have Bill Gates money in his bank account, but if this is not how you measure success, don't allow it to intimidate you.

Become the Best Version of Yourself: We spend a lot of our time comparing ourselves to others; this can only lead to one destination - and that is failure! When your focus is on what everybody else is doing, that is where you are putting your energy. However, when your focus is on becoming who you were created to be, what your sister or best friend are doing, will not affect you. When your focus is on yourself, you will inspire others to push themselves more.

We have a terrible habit of measuring our success according to our peers, if one of your friends is making more money than you, because of what the world has conditioned us to believe about success, we feel like a failure. In psychology, social comparison bias refers to the way we use comparisons to judge others. It makes it easier to make a judgment when we have a benchmark, and that is usually another individual. However, that does not mean that the judgment is accurate.

John Wooden was one of the most successful basketball coaches of all time. He believed that we measure success in the wrong way. Wooden proposed a compelling argument that success is not about what you have accomplished; it's about your accomplishments in comparison to your abilities. We can only become successful when we know that we have done everything in our capabilities to achieve our end goal. He went on to state that instead of having a grandiose outlandish dream, set your goals according to your reality and then do everything you can to achieve them. If you are unrealistic about your goals, you'll end up disappointed when you don't meet them, especially if you've put in the hard work.

Measure the Unmeasurable: It is easy to measure your finances; all you need to do is look at your bank balance. Most people would believe that Elon Musk is hugely successful, which is true; you can Google his name to find out what he has achieved. However, nobody knows what's going on inside his head. In July 2017, he sent out a tweet where he spoke about the level of stress that comes with the work he does. He mentioned that he has so many incredible moments, but when things are bad, they are so bad that sometimes the stress is unbearable. But people don't want to hear about that.

What we fail to realise is that there is no such thing as an easy life; no matter how wealthy you are, no matter how successful you get, you will never escape the trials of life. Because when you define success by your circumstances, and life takes a turn for the worst, you will not survive in the storm.

Measure Your Long-Term Results: There is no such thing as overnight success. When we look in the magazines, turn on the TV, or scroll through social media drooling over the glitz and the glamour, what you are looking at is the result. When you actually read the stories of famous leaders, entrepreneurs and superstar celebrities, you will find that every one of them went through hell to get to where they are today. Here are just a few examples:

Oprah Winfrey: I don't think there's a person in the world who wouldn't like to have her level of success; however, behind every great success, there is an even greater struggle. Oprah Winfrey was raised in abject poverty; she would wear potato sacks because there were times when her family could not afford clothes. She suffered a horrendous childhood and endured sexual and physical abuse for many years. She was raped by her 19-year-old cousin at the age of 9 and spent much of her life in turmoil.

Jim Carrey: Carrey is known for his gut-busting comedy; he has won countless awards, including the Teen Choice Awards, The Golden Globes, and The People's Choice, to name a few. And he is loved by millions worldwide; however, life has not always been this good. He was diagnosed with dyslexia in his early years and struggled at school; he was raised by a mother who battled with depression. When he moved to Canada, his family was so poor that they had to live in a Volkswagen camper for the first eight months of their time there. When he decided to leave Toronto and moved to Los Angeles to pursue his comedy career, things didn't go as planned. He struggled to find work; nobody would take him seriously as an actor, he was broke and destitute but refused to give up. His hard work paid off, he faced extreme adversity, but he chose to use his trials to propel him into greatness.

Steve Jobs: Steve Jobs was adopted as a child, in his later years he attended Reed College but dropped out after his first semester. Apple did not become popular overnight; he spent many years of his life not knowing what to do. When he finally founded Apple, he was sacked by the company that he established.

The point is that success takes time, and one of the reasons why people fail in life is because they expect immediate results. Take going to the gym, for example, many people will give up after the first few weeks because the six-pack hasn't developed, or the love handles haven't started dissolving.

One of the key drivers for success is momentum, all the small things that you do build-up, and you will eventually see the manifestation of all your hard work.

A great analogy to illustrate this is the Chinese bamboo tree. Once the seed has been planted in the ground, someone has to water and fertilise it every single day for four years. During that time, it appears as if nothing is happening, it hasn't started budding, and no leaves are appearing. The average person would see it as a waste of time. However, in the fifth year, all that work that went into feeding the seed four years prior manifests, and within six weeks, the Chinese bamboo tree grows to 90 feet! Whatever you are doing right now might feel like it's a waste of time, but what you are doing is watering the seed so that the roots are secure. If you have a big dream, you are going to have to put in a lot of work, and when the time is right, the opportunity will present itself to you, and you will be ready.

Les Brown is one of the best motivational speakers in the world, he was born with a severe learning disability, and he spent the majority of his life with extremely low self-esteem and self-limiting beliefs. He thought that he would never achieve anything in life because of his disability. Les Brown had one dream, and that was to become a disc jockey, one of his teachers encouraged him to believe in himself, and he carried those words with him for many years.

Despite having no experience as a disc jockey, Les Brown took the initiative to go and get some work experience at his local radio station. He spoke to the manager on the first day; there were no jobs available. He refused to take no for an answer, he went back the next day and asked if there were any jobs, once again he said no. He kept going back and speaking to the same manager, he received the same answer, but the last time he went the manager got so fed up with seeing his face that he told him to go and get him some coffee! That one tiny job led to another and then another within the organisation, Les Brown went to the radio station on a mission, and that was to become a disc jockey, he would practice his radio debut daily even though he had not so much as touched a microphone. One day, a disc jockey who had an alcohol problem was too intoxicated to go on air. After a series of events, Les Brown got his first slot on daytime radio. He had spent many years preparing for the opportunity, and when it came, he was ready.

Preparation is everything when it comes to success; however, it is during this time that most people give up, therefore, do not measure your success according to your current circumstances, measure it according to what you are working to become.

"Without self-discipline, success is impossible, period." Lou Holtz

How Can We Become More Successful?

Success is a target you've got to aim for, when we look at successful people, we assume that they have some inside information that only a select group of people have access to. Regardless of the circumstances you were born into; wealth is accessible to everyone if you want it enough. Some time ago, I saw a picture of bloody ballerinas' feet; the message spoke loud and clear. While everyone is admiring the ballerina for her excellent skill and talent, for her to master her craft in the way that she does, she has to put in hours and hours of practice; she has to go through an immense amount of pain and suffering. The problem is that people want the world, but they are not prepared to put in the work. This is why lottery companies are making so much profit because people would rather waste their money and attempt to take a short cut to wealth instead of doing what is required to become truly successful. There is a very specific formula to success, and if you follow it you will not fail, are there going to be bumps in the road? Are there going to be times when you want to give up? Of course, but persistence is the key to unlock the barriers in front of you. If you are going to become more successful, the first thing you will need is self-discipline. You will have heard that you need motivation for success. That is only one part of the equation; the first thing you need is self-discipline because even if you are motivated unless you have self-discipline, you won't be able to do what you need to do to become successful.

The Biology of Self - Discipline

There is a science to self-discipline, to understand how it manifests in your life, it is important to learn about its biological basis.

There are approximately 100 billion neurons in the human brain. Neurons are the tiny cells that produce our thoughts and behaviours. In 2009, Colin Camerer and Todd Hare used functional magnetic resonance imagining machines (fMRIs), to analyse the brain activity that occurs when people are participating in tasks that require the use of discipline and self-control. The participants were asked to decide whether they would accept a small financial reward immediately or a larger one in the future, the classic battle between willpower and delayed gratification. The study enabled them to determine that there was increased activity in two areas of the brain called the ventral medial prefrontal cortex and the dorsolateral prefrontal cortex when they were making decisions based on their immediate and future options. When choosing the option that had better long-term consequences, the activity in these areas was higher.

The findings of this study demonstrate that the ability to engage in self-discipline and make healthier long-term decisions is easier for some than it is for others based on the structure and activity of their prefrontal cortex. The results are incredibly significant because it helps us understand that people can not merely exercise self-control at will; you must develop it.

Self-discipline is strengthened when you continuously make healthy choices, but it is also diminished if you continually give in to unhealthy pleasures.

If you are the type of person who can never say no to a doughnut or finds it difficult to maintain a consistent exercise routine or wants to quit watching television every night and do something more productive, this is excellent news. It means that it is possible to improve; you are not doomed to failure.

A brain imaging study conducted in 2011 re-examined the participants of the Stanford Marshmallow Experiment (a very well-known study that was conducted 40 years prior). The study found that the original participants who were able to delay gratification had more active prefrontal cortices, as well as differences in the area of the brain linked to addictions called the ventral striatum when they were attempting to exercise self-control when faced with the decision of making unhealthy choices. Those in the delayed gratification group were also more successful in all areas of life in comparison to those in the immediate gratification group. The study revealed that a simple decision like whether or not to eat a marshmallow in the first years of life shaped their decision-making processes in adulthood.

There is no evidence to suggest that how much self-discipline a person has is determined by genetic predisposition or upbringing and environment. However, what we do know is that whatever level you are at, you can improve it. Lifting dumbbells strengthens the arms, and if you target those areas of the brain identified in the studies, they will also become stronger.

I want to encourage you as you are reading, not to feel disheartened if you suffer from a lack of self-discipline at this point in your life. It is easier to master specific skills in childhood, but that absolutely does not mean it is impossible to do so now. Willpower and self-discipline can be consistently exercised to achieve long-lasting results over time. All skills are the same; the more you practice, the better you become, discipline is no different.

Executive Functions and Focus

Your level of self-discipline is based on your ability to focus, and according to neuroscientists Paul Burgess and Jon Simons, focus is dependent upon a term referred to as 'executive functions.'

There are three executive functions crucial to self-discipline and impulse control: working memory, cognitive flexibility, and adaptability. Discipline requires that you are capable of setting goals, pursuing them, prioritising activities, controlling unhelpful inhibitions, and filtering distractions.

These functions occur in several brain regions, including the orbitofrontal cortex, the anterior cingulate cortex, and the dorsolateral prefrontal cortex. Just like with willpower and self-discipline, these are specific brain functions that you can target if you want to improve them. It is impossible to master self-discipline and focus separately, the two work hand in hand. Being disciplined means that you can consistently focus on what you need to do to accomplish your goals.

Willpower Fatigue

We do not have everlasting stores of willpower and discipline since they are biologically based, they run out when used. It's just the same as lifting weights; the muscles get tired after lifting. The brain of a person who resisted the cookie once is different from the brain of a person who resisted the cookie ten times. No matter how much willpower one person may have, if the temptation is continuously placed in front of them, it will only be a matter of time before they give in. It's impossible to run for a full 24 hours; eventually, you will get too tired and give up, will power is the same.

Social psychologist Roy Baumeister conducted a study in 1966 where he measured a phenomenon called willpower depletion. The study involved putting 67 participants in a room with freshly baked cakes and cookies, as well as some bitter radishes. One group had their willpower tested by being told to eat the radishes while the other group was allowed to indulge in the sweet treats. They were then moved to another location and given a puzzle to test their persistence. The radish eaters gave up faster than the group who were allowed to eat the sweet treats because their willpower was depleted in the previous task, and they were now ready to take the path of least resistance.

The human brain has evolved over the years, so that our daily survival is its top priority. Living in this modern era, we understand that temporary low energy levels and low sugar are not going to kill us, but biologically, the brain doesn't know this and will go into survival mode to protect you. And survival mode opens the door to instant gratification, binge eating, and other failures linked to a lack of self-discipline. Therefore, the most effective way of exercising self-discipline is to remove yourself from the situations that will lead to your failure.

If you are finding it difficult to stop eating unhealthy food, stop buying it and you will find that when it's not there, you won't eat it. Therefore, when you do your grocery shopping, avoid the aisles with the sweet treats and go straight to the healthy aisles. In this way, you only need to exercise your willpower for the short amount of time you are in the store, as opposed to trying to resist the temptation of eating the cookies in the cupboard every evening.

Another way to conserve your willpower is to go shopping after you've eaten a filling, healthy meal instead of when you are hungry. Hunger leads to snacking, so when you are in the store with an empty stomach, you are more likely to pick up a bag of chips to satisfy that craving than pick up an apple. In this way, you are creating conditions where you are not forced to try and use self-discipline when you are feeling vulnerable. A bad diet may not be your personal struggle, but the same concept of picking your battles wisely can be applied to just about any area of life when it comes to self-discipline.

Another biological factor that plays a role in willpower is stress. When we are under pressure, the body goes into fight or flight mode, and we are more likely to act irrationally and instinctively. Stress causes the prefrontal cortex to malfunction, making us more likely to focus on short-term outcomes, which leads to us making decisions we end up regretting.

The principle of discipline is relatively straight forward; as a fully functioning adult, you know the difference between right and wrong, you've just got to be consistent about choosing the right option consistently regardless of the immediate gratification you will get from choosing the wrong option. Having an awareness of discipline will help to make a difference. This book aims to make it as easy as possible for you to have a high level of self-discipline. Accomplishing this goal becomes more realistic when you are aware of the factors that will drain you of your willpower and putting yourself in circumstances that are most favourable to you.

Remember that there is a biological basis to discipline, and just like any other habit, it is hardwired into your brain when it is practised. Start taking baby steps to exercise the habit of discipline, and you will begin to have more success in your daily life. When the opportunity arises, you must choose discipline.

Increase Your Motivation

We have all experienced motivation, the energy you get after you watch an inspirational film, listen to a motivational speaker, hear motivational music or an inspiring story, you suddenly have the drive to go to the gym, to work on that assignment or to write that book, but a few days later that momentum is no longer there, and you slip back into old habits. You stop waking up at 5 a.m., you start having a doughnut for breakfast instead of a smoothie, or you stop riding the bike to work.

Everyone has experienced this at some point in their life; some people will argue that there's no point in being motivated if it doesn't last, and I will say that there are certain things you need to do every day to maintain it. For example, we need to take a shower every day, and we need to eat every day. If we were to fail to do these things, this world would be a pretty stinky and hungry place! Motivation works in precisely the same way, think about it for a moment, if you were motivated when you watch that film, it means that you can get motivated, and if it doesn't last, you've got to do something to get it back.

The difference between the rich and the poor is the rich motivate themselves daily, whereas the poor experience motivation once in a while and have nothing to drive them towards their goals. I will continue to stress; there is nothing easy about success; if it were everybody would be successful, it takes a specific mindset to accomplish goals. As human beings, we want to take the path of least resistance, which means if it doesn't feel good, we're not doing it.

Waking up at 5 a.m. doesn't feel good, saying no to social events doesn't feel good; eating salad for dinner every evening doesn't feel good. But if you're going to get anywhere in life, you must either do things that don't feel good or find a way of looking your task in hand that makes you feel highly motivated, energetic and raring to go. This is a technique called framing, and it is very common among many highly successful people and self-made millionaires.

That is the essence of discipline; don't leave it to others to motivate you, motivate yourself. I will discuss motivation in more detail in chapter 5.

What Affects Our Success?
When thinking about success, I realised that as a child, some of my teachers and adults had unknowingly misled me.

We are told to go to school to get an education and then get a career and work your hardest to become the manager of that company. It sounds good on the surface until you get into the workforce and realise that you are not happy, and most people are not satisfied because they have no passion for the job. I'm in no way knocking education, go ahead and get your degree; however, if you want to achieve real and lasting success, you need to change three things: your mindset, habits, and your actions.

Your mindset: How we perceive ourselves and the world around us directly influences what we do in life. Our actions rarely differ from our beliefs and the unique internal representations that each of us makes inside our own head.

For example, imagine you have to convince a room full of people to buy into your idea. With a negative mindset, you imagine stumbling through a difficult and uncomfortable presentation, nobody listening and being cut short before you had finished.

From 1 to 10, how much do you feel like being the room?

Now imagine going into the same room with a positive n expansive mindset. Envisage a room full of people who admire and respect you, itching to hear what you have to say.

From 1 to 10 now how much do you want to be in that room?

For centuries people were terrified to voyage too far in case they fell off the edge of the earth. Only when the Ancient Greeks began to prove that the world must be spherical did that particular fear begin to dissipate.

There is a self-fulfilling prophecy going on here. Our beliefs and perception of the world directly influence our actions.

What you think will determine your level of success. The negative or poor mindset will bring failure. The expansive wealthy mindset will bring success.

As simple as it sounds, controlling your thoughts is difficult; one of the reasons for this is that we don't realise what we are thinking most of the time. The majority of our thoughts are unconscious, and we are led by our subconscious mind. Anything you were taught to believe as a child is what drives you today, so if you were raised in a family that operated with a scarcity mentality, and all you heard every day was, "Sorry we can't afford this, and we can't afford that, we can't afford to send you to college, we can't go on this vacation, and we need to be more frugal with our money." That is now your general mentality when it comes to wealth.

The only way to overcome this is to recognise that your thought process does not line up with your desires.

When you arrive at this conclusion, you are ready to start moving forward because you can change your mindset and begin thinking of success instead of poverty. You will experience a radical transformation in your life and your circumstances.

Habits: I will discuss this further in chapter 4; however, it is important to mention at this point that your habits will determine your level of success. Whether they are good or bad we all have habits, the difference between successful people and unsuccessful people is successful people cultivate good habits that lead them to success, and unsuccessful people cultivate bad habits that lead them to failure.

Actions: Although the actions you take are what ultimately determines your success, your actions are actually determined by your mindset and your habits. Your habits will affect the actions you take towards your dreams. If you believe that people who become wealthy only do so because they are lucky, and you have poor habits such as of coming home every evening and watching reality TV, then you are never going to become successful.

Success requires that you take massive action to achieve your goals, and that means developing discipline, motivation, determination and many of the other habits we will be discussing shortly if you are really serious about changing your life.

2. How You Value Time Will Hugely Affect Your Success. Period!

"The rich invest in time, and the poor invest in money."

Warren Buffet

We are all given 24 hours in a day, for most of us, eight of these hours are spent asleep, we are then left with 16 hours to achieve our goals. Time is a valuable asset: when you lose it; you can't get it back. You can lose all your money and make it again. If you were sick, you can get healthy again. But when you waste time, you cannot get that back.

Here's the key point: **what you choose to do with your time is of great significance, and the self-made rich view time very differently to the masses.**

What is Time?

No matter what part of the world you live in, everybody is familiar with time. Science, religion, philosophy, and the arts all have their definitions of time. However, the system of measuring it appears to have some inconsistency. Clocks are based on hours, minutes, and seconds. Throughout history, the basis for these units have changed, but the concept is rooted in ancient Sumeria. But when it comes to defining time, there does not appear to be a concrete answer.

According to physicists, time is related to how events progress from the past to the present and into the future. They believe that time does not change. Time is not tangible, we cannot taste touch or see it, but it is something that we can measure. In the natural world, time moves in one direction; this is referred to as the arrow of time. An unanswered question in science is whether time is reversible? One explanation is that we live under the laws of thermodynamics, which suggests that time either remains constant or it increases. In other words, we can never go back in time.

Classical mechanics suggest that time is the same everywhere; However, according to Einstein, time is relative. It depends on the observer and the frame of reference. Relativity can lead to time dilation, which is when the time between events extends the closer an individual travels towards the speed of light.

Clocks that move operate slower than stationary clocks; this effect becomes more prominent as the moving clock draws closer to the speed of light. Clocks in orbit or aeroplanes move slower than clocks on earth.

However, there are several problems with the idea of travelling back in time. One Issue is related to cause and effect, which can lead to what is known as a temporal paradox. One example of this is called the 'grandfather paradox,' which states that if you were able to travel back in time and take your grandfather's life before the birth of your mother or father, you would stop your own birth. Most physicists believe that it is impossible to travel back in time. However, they believe there is a solution to this, and that is the travel between two parallel universes.

The human brain is built to keep track of time, the brain can speed up or slow time down depending on the neurons fired. Everybody has heard the expression, 'time flies when you're having fun,' and according to scientists, this is because certain chemicals in the brain will cause neurons to fire at a certain speed depending on the events that are taking place. You find that when there is an emergency or danger, time slows down. According to scientists at the Bayer College of medicine in Houston, this is because there is an increase in the activity of the amygdala, the part of the brain where memories are formed.

According to science, time started when the big bang occurred; the question then becomes if time had a beginning, is there an end?

How the Masses View and Value Time
Regardless of the scientific arguments surrounding time, there is one thing that we do know; you cannot reclaim the time that you have wasted. We live in a world that is full of distractions, from television to social media to friends and family. However, your ability to minimise these distractions will determine whether you achieve your goals or not. There is a big difference between the way highly effective people view time and the poor view time.

How the Masses View Time

In chapter 1, I mentioned that 1% of the population owns 99% of the world's wealth. Time management is one of the reasons for this.

They Watch Too Much TV: According to research, the average American spends five hours each day watching TV! That adds up to 77 days per year! Just think about what you could achieve if you had an extra 77 days? There's nothing wrong with watching television but spending 25% of your day in front of a box is unacceptable!

They Waste Time on Entertainment: Again, there's nothing wrong with taking the time out to relax and enjoy yourself by participating in hobbies and activities that you find fulfilling. However, when you would rather pick up a gossip magazine, or read through a tabloid newspaper, or spend hours speaking on the phone about the latest office gossip, you are wasting your time. You will not find successful people wasting their time and mental energy on activities that do not enhance them.

They Waste Too Much Time on Social Media: According to a study conducted by entrepreneur James Chorley, 74% of poor people spend more than one hour each day on the internet engaged in recreational activities. Ninety-five percent of these respondents stated that they use sites such as Facebook to catch up on the latest entertainment, whether it's about friends or celebrities.

Only 37% of the wealthy in his study spent more than an hour a day taking part in recreational activities online. And out of this percentage, only 17% use sites such as Facebook for recreational purposes. They typically use social media platforms as a way of networking to build additional wealth.

"A man who dares to waste one hour of time has not discovered the value of life." Darwin

How the Wealthy View and Value Time

You will never hear a wealthy person say they don't have enough hours in the day because they do not view and value time in the same way as the masses. A common trait of the rich is that they view, value and guard their time, much like a traveller would value his water bottle when crossing the desert. They place a high value on their time and use it sparingly.

"The question I ask myself like almost every day is, 'Am I doing the most important thing I could be doing?' Mark Zuckerberg

Thomas Chorley conducted a study of 177 self-made millionaires over five years. He found that almost 50% of them woke up a minimum of 3 hours before the start of their workday. When everyone else is asleep, high achievers are up working. This strategy eliminates distractions; you see, it's not that we don't have enough hours in the day, it's just the hours that we should be using productively are spent asleep or doing unproductive activities. How many of you get frustrated at the end of the day when you realise that several things on your to-do list have been left unticked? Rising early allows you to complete the most important tasks of your day.

Rich People Buy Time: Yes, I know I have already said you can't buy time, but I didn't mean it in the way you are thinking. You can't buy back the time that you have wasted, but you can free up time to do the most important things, and you can do this by hiring people to take on tasks that will decrease your level of productivity. The easiest way to do this is to figure out the tasks you are taking on that waste time.

Let's say you earn £200,000 a year at your business or job. If you work 40 hours a week you are earning around $100 an hour, so any task that could pay a person less than $100 an hour would give you additional time to take on other projects for $100 an hour. Instead of mowing the lawn for 3 hours, pay one of the local teenagers to do it for $15 an hour. If you work for three hours while he is mowing the lawn you've made yourself $255, and if you have enough money already, you can spend three hours doing something that you enjoy like spending time with your family or indulging in one of your hobbies, the choice is yours.

Rich People Plan Their day: It takes an incredible amount of self-discipline to ignore daily interruptions. Successful people create a schedule for the day and break their workflow down into manageable tasks, but they follow them down to the very last minute. They remove distractions and focus on one task at a time.

How do you value your time?

To discover how you value your time, I have developed a short test that will take you no more than 3 minutes. The test is on the Wealthy Habits Cheatsheet available for free download at – juicypublishing.net/habits. If you don't have access to the online test, I have repeated the same questions below.

The test looks at some of the most common habits of highly productive and successful people. Please don't be disheartened if you answer 0 (or NO) to most or even all of these questions. The aim is simply to give you an indication of how you are currently valuing your time.

Score 1 for yes, 0 for no.

A score of 0-3 and you probably undervaluing your own time. A score of 4-5 is good, though you can certainly improve your productivity and the value you place on your time. Score 6-8, whilst there is still room for improvement, you likely place a high value on your time. 9 or 10, you already place a high value on your time and practice many of the habits and routines of highly successful people.

1. Do you avoid reality and non-educational TV?
2. Do you limit non-work related social media and email to once a day?
3. Do you delegate 3 or more major task at least once a day?
4. Two flights - one arrives at 3pm, the other at 3am but costs $20 less. Would you buy the expensive flight?
5. Do you have a daily exercise regime that gives you an endorphin high?
6. Do you use free time like a commute or waiting rooms productively?
7. Do you have go-to contacts for informed advice?
8. Do you mute phone and email alerts to avoid non-essential interruptions?
9. Do you regularly socialise with stimulating people who can help you achieve your goals?
10. Do you frequently say NO when someone asks you to do a worthless task?

It is important to remember that this test is in no way diagnostic and intended as a rough indicator of how you may be valuing your time. Whatever your score, adopting the techniques and ideas in this book will help improve your effectiveness and productivity, so let's read on.

3. Tried and Tested Ways to Free up Your Own Time

"Time is what we want most, but what we use worst." ~
William Penn

What are your reasons you want to improve your time management skills? Reasons drive your actions. Furthermore, your reasons need to be compelling enough to encourage you to keep going even when you encounter obstacles.

For example, let's say that you want to start making exercise a part of your daily routine; this would require you to begin waking up earlier to get your workout in. If you don't have a reason as to why you want to start exercising, I can guarantee that you will give up at some point (I am speaking from experience here). Just having a reason is not enough; it needs to be something that is going to motivate you to want to change your life.

You may have decided to start exercising because you watched a motivational film such as 'Rocky,' that's a great reason to want to hit the gym, but when you're not feeling well, when you're tired, or when you're feeling lazy that is not going to be enough motivation to get you off the couch. Why, because the reason is not compelling enough. But what if you've experienced a health scare such as the doctor telling you that you are a borderline diabetic, and if you don't change your eating patterns or start exercising, you will become a full-blown diabetic by the end of the year?

Your health is a serious enough reason for you to start exercising because your life is at risk if you miss a day of exercise, or you give in to a fast-food craving, the fact that you know that your health is at risk will motivate you to get back on track.

Now let's get back to the conversation about you wanting to start valuing your time more. Wanting to be more productive isn't enough; it sounds good because who wants to be less productive? Your goal of wanting more time to become more productive is not enough to spark the motivation required to achieve your goals. You've got to get even more specific. Ask yourself how your life would change if you were more productive in your everyday tasks. To get you thinking about this, here are some ideas:

- To eliminate more stress
- To get better sleep because you are experiencing less stress
- To increase my income but work fewer hours
- To increase the amount of time I spend with my family

These goals are general; however, yours are going to be a lot more specific to you. When you break your goals down in this way, you give yourself more reason to achieve them.

Time Wasting Behaviours

Before you go to bed at night and you analyse the events of your day, you probably add to your stress levels by thinking about all the things that you have not achieved. Typically, the reason for this is that you spend a lot of time doing things that steal your time and prevent you from getting the most important things done. Here are some examples of time-wasting behaviours:

Failing to Plan: When you don't spend enough time in preparation, you are forced to spend additional time in execution. The time you invest in compiling, collecting, and organising your thoughts before the start of the project wastes time. Planning is useful because the process helps eliminate problems or roadblocks before you begin working on the project. It is also a way for you to imagine how you are going to perform the task so that you can think of ways to become more efficient.

Proper planning is a tool you should use for all tasks, not just large ones. Spending 10 minutes at the end of a workday to take a look at your schedule and plan out the materials you will need to increase effectiveness and productivity the following day will improve efficiency.

Multitasking: Everybody knows somebody who takes great pride in their multitasking skills (maybe you are that person). However, research suggests that switching back and forth between tasks is an ineffective way of getting things done. When you work on one project at a time, you are forcing your brain to switch to a different memory experience and skill set, meaning that you can't put your full effort into each task.

One study found that when people who spoke two different languages were asked to count objects by switching between the languages they spoke, between each switch, they had to slow down even when it came to their most fluent language. Another study found that when we stop and start between projects, it increases the time required to complete each task by as much as 500%!

There are times when multitasking is required; for example, you may be cooking dinner at the same time as telling one of your children where to find their socks, at the same time as helping another child with their homework. Or, you may be listening to jazz, reading a book, and occasionally responding to your partner who is reading a book at the same time. However, these tasks and projects do not require that You focus to achieve the best outcome

Spending Time with Negative People: The average person would not consider this as time-wasting behaviour. However, you will find that when surrounded by negative people, they lower your energy levels, slow your productivity, reduce your enthusiasm, and leave you feeling drained. The more you separate yourself from negative people, the easier it will be to accomplish your goals.

Daydreaming: This is another underrated time-wasting behaviour. Many of us can spend hours thinking about the life we want. It is important to mention that there is nothing wrong with visualising your success; however, if you spend more time thinking about it, then doing something about it, you have a problem.

Repeating Conversations in Your Mind: The brain tends to bring up events and situations that did not go according to plan. In these moments, we can waste time thinking about what we should've said, what we should've done, how we should've done it, etc. Repeating conversations is a pointless activity; the event or situation is in the past; there is nothing you can do to change it. Resolve in your mind that you won't make the same mistake again and forget about it.

Being a Perfectionist: There is no such thing as perfection; it doesn't exist. When you devote too much time to a task because of your unrealistic high standards, you waste time. Even if you have completed the job, you continue making revisions in the hopes that it will be perfect. Spending hours going over a project until you think you have eliminated every mistake is a massive time-wasting activity.

Working Backward: This is a form of procrastination; most people will put the most difficult tasks to one side and get the easy ones out of the way first (see Eating the Frog in chapter 4).

Working backwards is not the way to build momentum. First of all, when you know that you've got to work on a project that you dread, you are unconsciously going to work slower on the more manageable projects. Second, saving the worst until last usually results in you putting it off again until the next day.

Now that I've given you some insight into time-wasting behaviours, let's think about habits you are indulging in that are stealing your time.

At this point, I would like you to get a pen and paper and write down every habit you believe is preventing you from being more productive. You can use a blank piece of paper, or section 2 of the <u>Wealthy Habits Cheatsheet</u>.

Replace Bad Habits with Good Ones.
There is a reason why you have bad habits, even though these behaviours are negative, they provide a benefit for you. Outside of time-wasting behaviours, let's say you had an addiction to cigarettes, every time you smoke, you do so because it makes you feel better, even though it's a negative habit and will eventually damage your health. Or, you may be in a bad relationship, but because it provides companionship, it is fulfilling your emotional needs. In some cases, a bad habit may be a way of coping with stress, for example, clenching your jaw, tapping your foot, pulling your

hair, or biting your nails. These are all ways in which bad habits act as a benefit to you.

You might have the bad habit of opening your inbox several times throughout the day. You may do so because it makes you feel connected to the outside world. Since bad habits have benefits, it is almost impossible to stop doing them. Instead, you must replace them with a new habit that provides a similar benefit. For example, if you turn on the TV as soon as you get back from work, the benefit may be that it relaxes you.

So instead of trying to eliminate that habit, replace it with something that will help you relax when you get back from work. The good habit could be meditation or reading a book. It's up to you to decide what will provide a benefit of equal value, just ensure that it's not another bad habit that is going to continue stealing your time,

"Your net worth to the world is usually determined by what remains after your bad habits are subtracted from your good ones." -Benjamin Franklin

How to Free up More Time

Adopting good habits is the first step towards improving your time management and getting the most out of your day.

Now you need to apply specific strategies that will assist in boosting productivity and maximising your time.

Avoid Digital Distractions: Smartphone devices are a blessing and a curse. People spend the majority of the time glued to their phones; even when a group of friends is out in public, everyone will have one eye on their phone at the same time as engaging in conversation. While you must remain connected to the outside world, you need to find a balance so that you can use your time constructively, and this involves creating boundaries. You can start by doing the following:

Disable Push Notifications: According to research, the average person receives approximately 45.9 push notifications on their smartphone each day. I do not need to tell you that this is a major productivity killer. The easiest way to prevent this interruption is to either turn your phone off altogether while you're working or disable your push notifications. Disabling your push notifications involves going through your phone apps and turning off all notifications apart from phone calls and text messages.

Create Digital Boundaries: Some entrepreneurs only check their phones when they're in the bathroom! Checking your phone while on the toilet makes perfect sense; it may not be everybody's cup of tea, but it eliminates you checking your phone when you should be doing the things that matter. If you want to know how much time you spend on different phone applications, check your screen time, and you will be shocked at the number of hours wasted scrolling through your phone. Your boundaries might include no checking your phone during working hours, or that you stop scrolling after 7 pm.

Organise Your Priorities: Take a look at your calendar; you will find that it's full of meaningless events. We don't realise how much time we spend doing things that don't count towards our end goal. This strategy ties in with learning to say "no" (discussed in chapter 4). When you go through your calendar and start crossing of nonessentials, it will require contacting some people and letting them know that you can't take part in this activity or help them with something that you have promised you would. This process will take a lot of courage, some people are going to be upset with you, but if you are going to succeed, you will need to make sacrifices.

Clean as You go: When you're are in a rush, the last thing you want to do is wash the dishes, it only makes sense to leave them in the sink to a later time. But what you will find is that you eventually spend more time washing up that pile of plates then if you had just cleaned up at the time. It also applies to mail; it is tempting to leave a stack of envelopes (especially when it is junk mail) on the table. Again, when you eventually do get around to tidying up you, spend more time trying to organise the mess that you have created than if you had of just cleaned up at the time.

"Let today be the day you give up who you've been for who you can become." Hal Elrod

On the surface, these might look like small changes, but over time you will find that they make a big difference.

At this moment, I want you to get your notepad or the <u>Wealthy Habits Cheatsheet</u> and make a list of the top 5 bad habits you would most like to break. These are the real shockers – this is where you are seriously wasting your time and unconsciously sabotaging your effectiveness and ability to generate wealth.

For each bad habit, write down the corresponding opposite success-generating habit that leaves you feeling motivated and improves productivity. You can do this either in a notebook or using Step 3 of Wealthy Habits Cheatsheet. If you do nothing else but eliminate these bad habits from your life, I promise that you are well on your way to a far more effective, motivated and successful you.

4. The Habits of Highly Successful People

"Depending on what they are, our habits will either make us or break us. We become what we repeatedly do." ~ Steven Covey.

Habits are routine behaviours we perform unconsciously. You don't need any motivation to get out of bed and brush your teeth in the morning, this is something we have been trained to do since childhood, and it is second nature to us.

You may not realise it, but some of you have a habit of coming home every evening and sitting in front of the TV. A friend's father used to do this when I was a child, as soon as he walked through the door, I knew his every move. He would come into the house, greet us in the living room, go upstairs, go to the bathroom, go back to his bedroom, take off his tie, come downstairs, dish some food, and then sit in front of the TV for the rest of the night. This was his routine Monday through Friday; it was a habit; he did it without thinking.

Your habits define your character because they become a pattern of behaviour that people identify you by. If your friends always expect you to be late, you have a bad habit of being late, you probably go to bed too late, wake up late, and that's how the cycle of lateness starts. Or you might have a bad habit of eating every time you are feeling stressed. According to psychologists, such habits are formed as a result of the link between a stimulus and a response. This is the mental connection between the thoughts that trigger an action, as this pattern is repeated over time, it forms into a habit and affects all decisions and actions. Unless a person makes the conscious decision to change it, this habit will become permanent. As you have read, wealthy people have different habits to the masses; here are some of them.

"The trick to success is to choose the right habit and bring just enough discipline to establish it." - Gary Keller and Jay Papasan

How the Wealthy Operate at Work

Wealthy people have a different work ethic to the average person. Not only do they work harder, but they also work smarter, here are some habits that will improve the way you work.

Avoid Meetings: We are all accustomed to meetings; it is the norm in any work environment. However, entrepreneurs such as Elon Musk and Mark Cuban do their best to minimise the amount of time they spend in meetings. Cuban believes that they are a complete waste of time; in one interview, he stated that the only way you can get him into a meeting is if you pay him. Elon musk encourages his employees to avoid meetings; he refers to them as a "blight" on large companies. In other words, they are a liability.

The above views are not just popular opinion; research suggests that meetings kill productivity. Although there are some benefits to meetings, like the opportunity to share ideas and collaborate on projects, they also have a negative effect on job performance.

Limit meetings to 10 minutes and make sure that everything you discuss during that time is related to your end goal.

The Eisenhower Matrix: This concept was popularised by former United States President Dwight D Eisenhower. In one of his speeches, he stated that he only has two kinds of problems, the urgent and important, this is how he organised his priorities and workload.

He understood that time management required efficiency as well as effectiveness; in other words, we must ensure that we work on the important things as well as the urgent. To do this and to limit the stress associated with having tight deadlines, it is important to understand the difference between the two:

- Important: These activities lead to the fulfilment of a goal, whether personal or professional.

- Urgent: These activities require our immediate attention, and they are typically linked to someone else achieving their goals. These are the tasks that we spend the majority of our time and effort on because of the consequences associated with not fulfilling these demands.

Once we have made a distinction between the important and the urgent tasks, we then have a clear direction about the things we need to give the most attention.

Always Carry A Notebook: Richard Branson carries a notebook at all times; this is because he has a desire to learn. When he experiences a reaction to something, he writes it down. The Greek shipping tycoon Aristotle Onassis gave the following advice:

"Always carry a notebook. Write everything down. When you have an idea, write it down. When you meet someone new, write down anything you know about them. That way, you will know how much time they are worth. When you hear something interesting, write it down. Writing it down will make you act upon it. If you don't, you will forget it. That is the $1 million question they don't teach you in business school!" Richard Branson

Check Emails Three Times Per Day: The average person checks their email 15 times per day. A study conducted by researchers from the University of British Columbia discovered that when people limit the number of times they check the email to three per day, their stress levels go down. Participants of the study found that they were able to focus on tasks that were most important during the day and meet deadlines. Overall, they felt that they accomplished more by limiting the amount of time they spent checking emails.

A survey of 5,242 leaders discovered that 78% of them checked their emails several times throughout the day, and 66% of respondents stated that the first thing they do in the morning is to check their email or their voicemail. Think about the consequences of this, let's say that you are working on an important project and it requires extreme concentration, every time you check your email you are breaking your concentration. You've then got to get back into focus mode to complete the task. The problem is that now you've given yourself an additional worry. At the back of your mind, you are thinking about the email you have just sent and whether that person has responded. As a result, you keep checking your emails to find out. And every time you take a break from your project, you are disrupting your ability to concentrate. The question is, how do we combat this?

You can start by taking a two-hour break from your email and during that time, focus on your most important projects even if you have to go to a better environment such as a coffee shop to get your work done.

Delegate Your Tasks: Delegation works well if you're self-employed or you run your own company. There are many tasks you can outsource to freelancers or your team to give you additional time to work on projects that are more important and will increase your earnings potential. For example, if your website has a blog, instead of writing the posts yourself, hire a copywriter to do so for you. Or instead of spending all your time making phone calls, chasing invoices, and doing administrative tasks, you can hire a secretary to do those things for you.

The Power of NO: One of the most valuable lessons I have learned is that no-one will prioritise or protect my time better than me. The majority of people act out of self-interest, they put their priorities first which makes sense because we are all responsible for making sure that our personal needs are fulfilled, nobody is going to do this for you. Furthermore, we must look after ourselves before anybody else, this concept makes some people feel uncomfortable, especially if you strive to be giving and loving in everything that you do. But when you keep putting others before yourself, the result is bitterness and resentment. I'm not suggesting you ignore the needs of others, and you are not there for friends, loved ones, and co-workers; however, you must be sensible with your time. When your life is in order, you are then free to help others.

Have you ever wondered why air hostesses give the advice that we are to put on our oxygen mask first in an emergency before helping anyone else? The aim of these instructions is not for self-preservation, but if you are in danger, how can you get somebody else out of danger? People who say "yes" to everything find it difficult to say "no" because they are not assertive; the good news is that assertiveness is something you can learn.

You are assertive when you have the self-confidence to pursue your own needs and express your wants even if you face opposition. It involves articulating your stance on a given topic without the need for validation or approval from others. For example, suppose you are discussing your religious beliefs with a friend. Being assertive means standing by your position regardless of whether your friend disagrees or not. It does not mean that you are argumentative; it means letting them know you believe what you believe, and nobody has the right to tell you otherwise. We all have people in our lives who make us feel guilty if we do not jump at their every command. These are the times when we must be assertive; it may cause offence in some cases; however, this is not your problem; if taking on a task is going to interrupt your life, say "no."

When you are assertive, it means allowing others to share their views and opinions, listening intently without interrupting before giving your point of view, and your thoughts are expressed with respect. When it comes to saying "no," it's not about giving people excuses until that person gets fed up and decides to do it themselves; it's about learning how to say "no" with grace and not feeling guilty about it. When your co-workers keep stopping by and asking for help, and you keep saying yes to their requests, by the time you realise the end of the day has arrived, and you haven't done anything. Or you're trying to get things done at the house, and your phone keeps ringing every 5-minutes. You can resolve situations like this by letting your co-workers know that they can only ask for assistance during a specific time and by telling friends and family members you're not available until a certain time or date if this means you have to shut your office door or turn your phone off then so be it!

Are you the type of person that says yes to every social event, and your calendar is always booked with random appointments that have nothing to do with your end goal? I'm not telling you not to socialise; however, keep it to a minimum, if you're going to succeed you must spend time working on your goals, and if it means that you are not going to see certain friends for a while that is the sacrifice you've got to make. Weigh up your options, what is more important to you, satisfying people, or achieving your dreams? It's a choice that you have to make; this one little word will change your life. Say "no" to everything that doesn't support your immediate goal. Fill your calendar with things that help you reach your goal and nothing else.

Practice gratitude: Joshua Lombardo-Bottema, CEO of GoWrench Auto, stated, *"The one habit I have found has really improved my business is gratitude. I practice gratitude in a variety of ways – I start off each morning thinking of all of the things I am thankful for, this helps me to get in the right mindset* *to really attack the day. I also practice gratitude often with my staff. I let them know they are appreciated and that they are doing a great job – this helps them to stay motivated and continue delivering their best. Gratitude has changed the culture of the company and the mindset of all those in it."*

In a 2016 study conducted by DeSteno and Dickens, they found that grateful people had more self-control. During the study, participants were asked to complete a task on the computer, when the computer broke down another individual who was part of the study assisted them. The researchers also measured patience, happiness, and self-control in the daily life of the participants for several weeks. Finally, they measured self-control by offering a greater financial incentive for completing the tasks if they waited for the money instead of receiving it immediately. The study found that there was a direct correlation between self-control and gratitude. People who had higher levels of gratitude were prepared to wait longer for the monetary reward than those with lower levels of gratitude. Here are a few strategies you can implement in your daily life to increase your levels of gratitude:

- Say Thank you More Often: There is no need to wait until someone does something for you, practice saying thank you to the people around you for the small things they do. If you have a partner, thank them for being fantastic, thank your friends for being awesome friends, thank your kids for being cute. However, don't just say thank you, really mean what you say because the aim here is to experience feelings of gratitude. So, when you thank someone, get into the habit of feeling that sense of appreciation.

- Have Gratitude Time: We can get so busy with the complexities of life that we rarely stop to sit down and think about the things we should be thankful for. So, whether it's the first thing in the morning or the last in the evening, schedule a few minutes to make a gratitude list. Get yourself a notebook and each day write down ten things that you are grateful for. Again, don't just write them down, really feel the sense of gratitude for each point on the list.

- Stop Complaining: We live in such a cruel and vicious world that it's easy to complain. You've only got to open the newspaper or turn on your TV or radio, and negativity bombards you. But when we moan and complain, we lower our vibrations, and it's difficult to experience gratitude because we are so focused on the negative.

How the Rich Behave with Money

Wealthy people do not work for money; they make money work for them. It is impossible to become wealthy with a 9-to-5 job; you must implement specific strategies if you want to see a turnaround in your finances.

Multiple Streams of Income: In a study conducted by entrepreneur Thomas Chorley, he found that 65% of self-made millionaire's had three streams of income. It makes sense to have more than one income source because when one is down, you still have money coming in from another avenue. The average person has one source of income, and that is their job; if you do not have an additional income stream and you lose that job, you won't survive. Therefore, you mustn't put all your eggs in one basket. Here are some examples of wealthy people with multiple streams of income:

- Arnold Schwarzenegger invests heavily in real estate.
- Warren Buffett has investments in 63 different companies.
- Elon Musk is the owner of seven businesses.
- Sir Richard Branson is the owner of more than 200 businesses.
- Mark Zuckerberg is the owner of 69 businesses.

Investments: Warren Buffett is known for investing in companies and holding onto them for several years before cashing out.

Get Financial Help: millionaires understand money in a way that the average person doesn't. However, they also have additional help from stockbrokers, tax consultants, and financial planners. These professionals ensure that their money works for them, it also helps them avoid expensive mistakes and stay on track of their finances

Tax Advantages: The wealthy take advantage of the system and make sensible investment decisions that work in their favour. When it comes to taxes, they leave their money in tax-deferred or tax-free funds like 401Ks, IRAs, or college 529 plans.

Invest in Real Estate: The wealthy own houses and land; they invest in tangible assets that increase in value over time and increase their earnings potential.

They are Frugal: One of the wealthiest men in the world Warren Buffett still lives in the same house he purchased in 1958 for $31,500. He has simple tastes that include Cherry Coca-Cola and McDonald's burgers. He has no interest in luxury cars or computers. He advises young people to stay away from credit cards - if you don't have the money don't buy it. Buffett's idea of luxury is not buying what the world says you should have but buy what you want.

Passive Income: As mentioned earlier, the rich make their money work for them; they have passive income streams, which means that they make money around the clock. It doesn't matter how many hours they are away from the desk finances continue to accumulate.

The Pareto Principle: The Pareto principle is also known as the 80/20 rule. The philosopher and economist Vilfredo

Federico Damaso Pareto discovered the concept. One day while in his garden, he noticed that 20% of his pea plants generated 80% of the healthy pea pods. It led him to start thinking about uneven distribution, and one of the things that he learned was that 20% of the population owned 80% of the land in Italy. He began to research different industries and found that 80% of the production generally came from 20% of the companies. He eventually concluded that 80% of results require 20% action; this became known as the Pareto principle. Even though the ratio is not always exact, it is an excellent rule of thumb widely used by successful people.

When applying this principle on a personal level, you will find there is an 80/20 principle to your habits. For example, you may own ten beautiful suits, but 80% of the time, you only wear two of those suits. You may own a whole shoe rack of classy heels, but you only grab the same 20%. You may live in a ten-bedroom home and spend 80% of your time in only a few rooms. I'm sure you get my point, so how can you use the Pareto principle to free up time? Find out which 20% of your work produces 80% of your income. When you work this out, that is where your focus should be.

Free time: Relax and let off steam like the rich and successful

In Stephen Covey's book, 'The 7 Habits of Highly Effective People,' he mentioned that one of the most underrated habits of successful people is taking the time out to rejuvenate, recharge and relax. Relaxation is one of the reasons why you find that so many wealthy people block out their calendars for regular trips to the spa. Society has conditioned us to believe that the only way you can be effective is if you work multiple hours for someone else. When you ask the average person what they do to relax, the majority will say they have no time for themselves because they're too busy. However, even though we are such a busy nation, in most cases, we are often busy building for somebody else.

Wealthy people understand that it's important to look after yourself; first, this is essential if you are going to perform at your best. Not only do highly effective people place a demand on themselves to excel, but they must also cope with high-pressure situations, which requires an extreme amount of physical stamina and mental agility. The wealthy will step back from a problem and recharge their batteries by spending time relaxing.

It is also important to spend time with family and friends. Again, this should be blocked out on your calendar as a repeated event. Many people have had to learn this the hard way. Multi-millionaire entrepreneur Dan Lok received a phone call from his mother saying that his father was sick in the hospital. He called his dad to ask if he was okay, his father replied that he had to have surgery and that he would be fine. Dan responded that he needed to close one last deal, and then he will make his way to the hospital. Unfortunately, Dan's father died shortly after that conversation, and he never got to see him again because of a business deal. Don't make the same mistake, life is precious, and you never know if you're going to see tomorrow. Therefore, spend as much time with your loved ones as you can.

Spend Time on Your Hobbies: We all have activities and things that we love to do. As a child, you might have enjoyed bike riding or mountain climbing, as you grew older, the pressures of life took over, and you stopped participating in these activities. Hobbies enrich your life, bring you joy, and give you something exciting to participate in during your leisure time. They also provide you with something else to focus your mind on other than the stresses of everyday life.

Go on Vacation: Going on vacation enhances your work-life balance. Research suggests that Americans work more hours than anyone in the industrialised world. Americans Retire later, work longer days, and take less vacation. Stress management and productivity trainer Joe Robinson the author of "Work to Live" and "Don't Miss Your Life," states there are several factors that drive this issue, at the top of the list is many companies are continually downsizing and making staff redundant. Employees do not want to take a vacation just in case they return to no job. Some are afraid that taking time off means they are not as committed as other workers.

Several studies conclude that taking time off from work can have psychological and physical benefits.

Physical Health: Stress contributes to high blood pressure and heart disease. According to the New York

Times, people who take a vacation every two years as opposed to every six years reduce the risk of heart attack or coronary heart disease.

Mental Health: Neuroscientists have discovered that exposure to excessive amounts of the stress hormone cortisol causes changes to the structure of the brain. Cortisol can contribute to conditions such as depression and anxiety. Time away from work induces feelings of calm and relieves stress; this allows the mind and body to heal in a way that is not possible when we are under pressure.

Overall Well-Being: A Gallup study found that those who make time to take regular trips had a higher well-being index in comparison to those who travelled less. Another study found that physical complaints, mood, and quality of sleep had improved in comparison to their levels before vacation and after vacation.

More Mental Power: After returning from vacation, people are more productive and focused. Studies have concluded that chronic stress causes problems with memory and stagnates the part of the brain that is responsible for goal-orientated activity.

Improved Relationships. A study conducted by the Arizona Department of health and human services discovered that women who talk about vacations were happier in their marriages.

Decreased Burnout: Workers who take time to go on vacation and relax experience less burn out. They return rejuvenated, refreshed, and ready to take on another workload. Spending time out of the office improves productivity.

Habits and Day-to-Day Routines of Incredibly Successful People

"Practice isn't the thing you do once you're good. It's the thing you do that makes you good." Malcolm Gladwell

Successful people perform the same habits every day; everything they do improves them physically, mentally, and spiritually.

The First Hour of the Day: What you do first thing in the morning will set the tone for the rest of your day, if you keep hitting the snooze button, fail to go on your morning jog and then get a junk breakfast, you are going to see your day as a failure and continue to operate in that mode. Your thought process will be something like, *"If I've already had junk for breakfast I might as well get a pizza for lunch, there's no point in me working out in the evening because I've already eaten all this unhealthy food, so I might as well start again tomorrow."* People build bad habits by failing to do the most important things in the morning. When you jump out of bed as soon as the alarm clock goes off, go for a run, come back home and have a healthy breakfast, you will feel so good that you will want to continue making healthy decisions throughout the day.

Your morning routine does not need to be elaborate, but there are some key habits successful people incorporate into their lives before they start work. For example:

- Barack Obama wakes up at 7 a.m. and exercises for 45 minutes before having breakfast and making his way to work
- Bill Gates wakes up at 4 a.m., works out on the treadmill at the same time as watching an educational DVD, he then has breakfast and gets to work
- Oprah Winfrey wakes up at 6 a.m., takes the dogs out, reads affirmations, and does meditation before she starts her day

Can you see the pattern here? Many famous and highly successful people have a specific morning routine that enhances their lives.

The Final Hour of The Day: You have read that what to do first thing in the morning defines your day, but what you do at the end of your day is equally as important. Sleep is essential for resting the mind, renewing the body, and recharging our batteries so that we can be productive the following day. A night-time routine that allows you to prepare for the following day and decompress is essential. Simple things such as reading and turning off screens is a way to relax and unwind to prepare you for a good night's rest. Most importantly make sure that you get at least seven hours sleep a night, not only does a lack of sleep kill your productivity, but eventually it is detrimental to your health.

Exercise Everyday: Exercise is a very effective way of improving your self-discipline; there are several reasons for this:

- It Forces You to Take Action: If you are serious about improving your level of self-discipline, you are going to do whatever it takes to get there. Exercise is a physical activity; you've got to move. As you move physically, you begin to move mentally; it builds that bridge from thinking to doing. When it comes to goal setting, people spend a lot of time thinking about the goal without actually doing anything to achieve the goal. Once you have removed the physical barriers, you will remove the mental ones that are holding you back from success.
- Exercise is a Daily Practice: Fitness is a daily discipline; if you want to stay in shape, you will need to keep working at it.
- Exercise is Constant Improvement: Once you start exercising, you will begin to notice a difference in your health. You will start getting stronger, and you will start looking better, this will motivate you to continue.

Practise Meditation: A group of Italian researchers studied the brains of participants who were new to meditation before and after completing an eight-week mindfulness course. They found that meditation strengthened the dorsolateral prefrontal cortex, which is the part of the brain responsible for will power. In other words, meditation helps you do the things you don't want to do. Taken from mindful.org, here are some simple ways you can start practising meditation:

- Find a comfortable place to sit and focus on your breath as you inhale and exhale
- Where is most of your breath coming from? Your nose or your stomach? Pay attention to this for two minutes

That's it, spend a few minutes per day focusing on your breath, and you will soon reap the benefits of meditation.

Eat a Healthy Diet: Eating a healthy diet should apply to you, whether you are overweight or not. Some people can eat fast food every day and stay slim, they might look good on the outside, but their insides are rotten. A bad diet makes self-discipline difficult because you don't have the energy to do anything. The body needs the right vitamins and essential minerals to function at its best; without them, you will find it difficult to perform physical and mental activities because the body becomes tired and sluggish.

Choose to eat plenty of vegetables and fresh fruits; be careful not to overcook your vegetables because it removes all the much-needed helpful nutrients. Spinach and red meat are rich in iron, and fish such as salmon and tuna are high in omega-three fats. Foods high in protein are a good source of energy; you will find it in nuts, beans, and lean meat. Your carbohydrates should consist of whole-grain pasta, rice, or bread for additional fibre.

A healthy dinner plate should contain a large portion of vegetables, whole grains, protein, and fruit. The more energy you have, the easier it will be to achieve your goals.

Work from a Calendar NOT a To-Do List.

Most of us believe that a useful time management tool is to write a to-do list and that calendars are used to schedule appointments. Successful people do not operate like this; they use calendars to schedule everything. If you were to map out your ideal work week, you would find there are reoccurring themes, for example, hobbies, time to relax, family, exercise, etc. Getting rid of your to-do-list and making your tasks appointments is the best way to design your life and stay consistent.

With a to-do list, you'll find that nothing ever gets done, you write down what you need to do for the week. Still, at the end of the week, you failed to achieve several things you then put them onto the next week, and the same pattern begins. When you use a calendar, you are less likely to keep putting things off.

Using a calendar for time blocking enables you to look at your life's priorities weekly. Research suggests scheduling tasks on a calendar instead of using a to-do list will increase cognitive performance, reduce stress, and free your mind.

It is also important to schedule time on your calendar to do nothing. LinkedIn CEO Jeff Weiner states that he has several greyed-out blocks on his calendar where nothing is scheduled. To become more productive, he ensures that he spends time detached from his work life so he can recharge his batteries and get back to business with even more motivation.

If you don't take time out, you will reach burnout some people suffer from exhaustion and other health issues, if you don't take a break, you will get to the point where you are forced to take time out. Schedule days of nothing into your calendar and make it a consistent part of your routine.

Eat the Frog: The term 'eat the frog' was popularised by Mark Twain; he believed if you start your day by eating a live frog, you can get through the rest of your day knowing that the worst thing that is going to happen has happened. Your frog is your largest, most challenging, and most important task, it is the one that you are most likely to want to ignore and that you will spend time procrastinating on. But discipline yourself to complete the most difficult task first so that you are free to move on with everything else.

The key to achieving high levels of productivity and performance is to cultivate a lifelong habit of doing major tasks first thing in the morning; in other words, develop a habit of eating your frog first. Don't spend time thinking about it, wondering how you're going to do it, just do it. Many successful CEOs have adopted this strategy, and it is considered an essential leadership quality. Effective and successful people are elbows in at the deep end when it comes to major tasks. They discipline themselves to work single-mindedly and steadily until they have completed those projects.

Eliminate Distractions

Distractions are things that cause us to take our attention off the main goal. There are several things you can do to eliminate distractions.

Minimize Decisions: Open Mark Zuckerberg's wardrobe, and you will find that he has a row of Albury t-shirts; if you open Barack Obama's wardrobe, you will find that he has a selection of grey or blue suits with blue ties. The manager of the most successful hedge fund in history, Ray Dalio, wears the same suit to work every day. The average person will look at them and wonder why people with so much money are wearing the same clothes all the time? The answer is that successful people want to limit their number of daily decisions. You need willpower to focus, to be creative, and make decisions. As you have read, willpower is limited; when you are always making decisions that are not important, it limits your performance. In an article with Vanity Fair, Barack Obama stated, *"I'm trying to pare down decisions, I don't want* *to make decisions about what I'm wearing and what I'm eating because I have too many decisions to make."*

The average adult makes about 35,000 decisions a day.

Mark Zuckerburg made similar comments, "I really want to clear my life to make it so that I have to make as few decisions as possible about anything except how to best serve my community."

I'm not saying that you need to swap your wardrobe out for a load of grey t-shirts, but there are things you can do to simplify your life, so you make fewer decisions:

- Start by spending a week making a note of the decisions you make every day
- Evaluate the decisions you make and determine whether they have any effect on your end goal; you will find that most of them don't
- Cut down your wardrobe; you will find that you have more clothes than you wear. Most of us waste time staring at a pile of clothes thinking about what to wear, and then we choose to wear the same clothes. Get rid of the clothes you don't wear
- Rotate your meals, instead of thinking about making a different meal every day, eat the same few meals throughout the week
- Decide what you need to do the night before instead of getting up in the morning and thinking about what you need to get done for the day. Sort that out the night

before so that when you wake up, you are ready for action

Use the Pomodoro Method: The Pomodoro method is an effective way to improve your productivity; marketing consultant Greg Head explains that the Pomodoro technique helps to train the brain to work in spurts for efficient concentration and work output. It gives you the discipline to become hyper-focused and power through distractions. The technique was developed in the early 1990s by entrepreneur, author, and developer Francesco Cirillo. He used a tomato-shaped timer to track his studies as a University student. Here is how you can get started with the Pomodoro method:

- Set a timer for 25 minutes
- Work on the task until the alarm goes off
- Put a tick on a sheet of paper
- Take a five-minute break
- And then repeat the process
- After four Pomodoro's take a longer break

The longer break is typically around 15 to 30 minutes, but you can take as long as you need to recharge your batteries before starting another 25-minute work session. It is important to mention that you cannot entertain distractions; however, there are going to be times when you don't have a choice. When this happens, stop your timer and attend to the distraction. Otherwise, you can implement what Cirilo refers to as the inform, negotiate, and call back strategy:

- Inform the person who has distracted you that you are in the middle of something and you will call them back
- Negotiate the time that you can get back to the individual
- Once you've completed the Pomodoro, go and tackle the issue

Make One Improvement: Fred Schebesta, CEO and co-founder of finder.com, shares, "My daily habit is to make one improvement every single day. Every morning when I wake up, I decide what that will be and how I'm going to implement it. The improvement might be regarding my business, my health, and wellness or my relationship with my daughters, but every day, I'm striving to be a little better than the day prior.

Thinking about what I am going to improve may not take longer than 10 minutes, but the implementation timing can vary. If it's a bigger goal, I will chunk it down into small bits that can be executed each day.

Doing this religiously every single day for at least the last ten years has seen me expand my business, grow my wealth, improve my relationships, and have a huge impact on my overall personal development."

The Three Things that Successful People do Before 8 am

As you have read, wealthy people have several habits that cultivate success. Here are three of them:

11. **They meditate/pray:** In every religion, meditation and prayer is a top priority, even if you are an atheist, and you do not believe that there is a higher power. People from all backgrounds have discovered the benefits and use them to wind down, relax and improve their personal lives.

    The medical field has determined that meditation is an effective way to reduce stress and deal with pain management. Research suggests that meditation improves brain function and memory; according to Benjamin Neal, Meditation is used in the classroom to help children concentrate and focus, artists actors and innovators use it as a way of getting in the zone of boosting creativity.

    Actors Cameron Diaz, Hugh Jackman, Tom Hanks, Kristen Bell, And Jennifer Aniston all use meditation during their daily routines. Authors Tony Robbins, Tim Ferris, comedians Steve Harvey, Jerry Seinfeld, Ellen DeGeneres, singers Katy Perry, Paul McCartney, and Sheryl Crow all use meditation to prepare them for the day.

Oprah Winfrey spends a minimum of 20 minutes per day meditating. She claims that when she's in this state that she can produce her best work.

Meditation is the cornerstone for success; it is where you receive inspired ideas to live your best life.

12. **They Spend Time Reading:** The most common item on a wealthy person's bed stand is a book. In fact, in the homes of wealthy people, it is the norm for them to have an entire library. Leaders are readers; if you want to earn more today, you've got to learn more. A wealthy person would rather spend $30 on a book then entertain themselves by going to watch a movie. During an interview, when Warren Buffett and Bill Gates were asked what superpower they would have if it were possible, they both responded that they would love to be able to read super fast.

One of the major keys to success is continuous education; your personal development determines your level of success. If you don't learn, you won't grow; some people say they don't like reading, well in this day and age you do not have an excuse not to pick up a book because today we have things like audiobooks that enable you to listen to informative content while you are driving doing housework, or working out. If your home is full of gossip magazines, this speaks volumes about your mindset. However, if the books you read are focused on your goals, it is evidence that you are serious about achieving them.

13. **They Write Down and Review Their Goals:** A study conducted in 1979 at Harvard Graduate School found that the 3% who wrote down their goals earned ten times as much as the 97% that didn't.

These results provide us with evidence that writing down your goals is one of the most important factors when it comes to achieving them. According to Actor and Life Coach Tony Robbins, setting goals is the first step in turning the invisible into the visible.

5. Proven Techniques to Help You Adopt Success-Generating Habits

"I've learned that champions aren't just born, champions can be made when they embrace and commit to life-changing positive habits." Lewis Howes

Go to your local fast-food joint or cook something healthy; workout at the gym or lay in; hit the snooze button or get up and start working on your goals. I could go on, but I think you get my point. There are things that we can't control like the weather, what somebody else is thinking, our family members - and there are those things that we can control.

It is the choices you make in life that will determine whether you succeed or fail.

You have the power to choose what you are going to do with your life; you are responsible for it. You can make every excuse under the sun as to why you are not where you should be, *"I didn't come from a rich family," "I was bullied in school," "I don't have the right education,"* your reasons are irrelevant because there are just as many people who have experienced much worse, but they managed to beat the odds and become successful, why? Because they chose to!

Everything in life is about choices and consequences if you choose to do the right thing, there is a positive consequence, but if you choose to do the wrong thing, there is a negative consequence.

You know the goals that you have set for yourself, and if you are going to achieve them, you must actively make choices about how you are going to arrive at your final destination.

Let's say you've always wanted to write a book; you have a great idea in your head, it's just a case of putting it on paper. Days go by; weeks go by, months go by, years go by, and this book has not been written. It's never too late to accomplish your dreams; however, there will come a time when you are going to have to make a choice between two types of pain, the pain of the discipline associated with this mammoth task, or the pain of regret that you will experience because your vision never came to pass.

The choice is yours!

If you decide to write the book, you will need time to do so, which means that there are some leisure and social activities you will have to forfeit. You are not going to like giving up your social life to pursue your dreams; it will hurt, but that pain will be temporary. Once you have determined your writing schedule, stick to it, there are days when you are not going to enjoy it, and sometimes, you are going to have zero motivation, but you must persevere.

You also have another option, and that is not to write your book and continue doing what you've always done. By not writing the book, you are not pushed out of your comfort zone, and you will protect yourself from possible failure. However, you will have that voice at the back of your head, just wishing you had enough discipline to write the book. You will never know whether those dreams of you becoming the next Steven King would have come true.

You are going to feel a little depressed when you first start thinking about life like this because you've realised that your life is your responsibility. But when it hits home that what drives your life is the vehicle of choice, you will begin to feel empowered. You will feel as if you are in the driver's seat, knowing that you can control the outcome.

This is what it means to be a responsible adult. When you begin to appreciate the fact that there is no easy way out and that you must be disciplined enough to walk on the path that is going to lead to your chosen destination no matter what sacrifices you need to make to get there.

Everybody has got that one friend or family member who believes that there is no point in trying because the entire world is out to get them, that murphy's law is waiting on every corner so no matter what they do, they are doomed to failure. People with this mindset are often depressed and anxious because when you believe that you have no control over the things that happen to you, there doesn't seem to be any point in living.

In the 1950's psychologist, Julian Rotter pioneered a theory called "the locus of control". He attempted to explain why there are some people who can look within and take responsibility for their life circumstances and why there are others who look for someone or something to blame.

Rotter referred to a "locus" as a place where things happen; the locus of control is the individual's perception of what controls the events that take place in their life, therefore, influences how they react.

When you have an external locus of control, you perceive life as something that happens to you. Even if you are living the life of your dreams, you believe that some external forces are taking the reins behind the scenes. For example, a person who gets top marks on an exam will attribute their success to a lenient marker or easy exam questions instead of the fact that they spent day and night preparing for the exam. On the other hand, when you have an internal locus of control, you believe that you have played an active role in all the events that have taken place in your life. Using the exam example, you accept that your intelligence and study habits got you the best grades.

Self-discipline becomes a lot easier when you operate from an internal locus of control. Not only do you believe that it is your responsibility to make the right choices, but when you do, and you reap the rewards because of it, you accept that you deserve to take the credit. Such people enjoy developing a plan of action and carrying it out because they know it's going to get them the results they want. However, when a person with an external locus of control lacks self-discipline, it's dangerous because they believe that they are responsible for their lives but cannot enforce their plans. This is a bad place to be in because it leads to self-blame.

Tips for Successful Habit Execution

When it comes to self-discipline, the navy SEALs have mastered it. SEAL stands for Sea, Air, and Land, and those who become SEALs are some of the most consistent, skilled, and disciplined people on the planet. Becoming a SEAL requires extensive training and the majority of soldiers who start the training program drop out very early on.

Those who do complete it understand that the mind is the most powerful weapon known to man, they are equipped with the mental fortitude and the physical strength to achieve any mission they are assigned no matter how difficult.

The 40% Rule: One of the strategies that the Navy SEALs implement is the 40% rule; it states that when the mind begins to tell a person that they are exhausted and can no longer continue; in reality, they have only reached 40% of their full capacity. This means that if they choose to believe it, they have another 60% left in them. When you think you can't go any further, you still have a long way to go before you are completely depleted. To believe this, you must accept the physical and mental pain you are enduring at that moment.

Most people are ready to give up as soon as they feel the burn; this is only touching the surface of our boundaries.

The key to unlocking your remaining potential is to push through the pain and the voice in your head telling you it's time to quit. When you have a strong belief in yourself, and you can push past those pain points, it builds mental toughness and confidence. For example, after doing ten crunches, you start to hear a voice in your head that you are too tired, too weak, and too sore to continue. But if you take a break for a couple of seconds and then continue, you've already proved to that voice that you can continue. Then you pause again and do another, and before you know it, you've done 20 crunches. You had to take it slowly, but you've just doubled what you initially thought was possible.

When you believe that you can do more, it becomes your reality, and you will do more.

Belief allows you to push past the limitations you have erected in your mind, and once you overcome the urge to give up the first time, the next time you are challenged, you will know that you are capable of accomplishing whatever task has been set before you. This is the essence of self-discipline, it's about endurance, but most of us are not willing to go past a certain point.

When we believe that we are capable of something, our mind becomes our best friend; but when we believe we are incapable, it becomes our worst enemy. You've got to choose to empower yourself using the 40% rule instead of throwing in the towel at the first hint of resistance.

Think about this for a minute; you decide to run the marathon even though you haven't practised, and you are not physically fit enough to do so. While you are running, you won't be able to catch your breath, your legs will start feeling weak, and you will begin to wonder whether this was a good idea. At that moment, you could give up and save yourself the agony of completing the marathon. But if you were running because someone was chasing you and your life was in danger, no matter how much pain you were in, you would keep running because your life depended on it. The reality is that the majority of us have no idea of our true mental and physical capabilities.

We have become complacent, our jobs pay just enough money to pay the bills, or we can buy a larger clothing size and convince ourselves that we don't look that bad. Because we don't challenge ourselves, we have no idea what we could achieve if we did. It's only those who choose to become extraordinary that master discipline. That's one of the reasons why people love watching sports so much; there isn't anything that great about watching a group of men bounce a ball up and down a court. But that's not really what people are paying attention to, what they admire is the player's ability to master their craft. It's easier to watch someone else become an expert than to become an expert yourself.

Several studies have proved that mental strength plays the most important role in our physical abilities. Most notably, the placebo effect, which is when an individual's performance is enhanced because of the belief that something that they have done will impact their performance. In 2008 the European Journal of Neuroscience published a study that found participants who believed sugar pills were caffeine worked harder during a weightlifting session. The belief that they would have extra energy and strength enabled them to tap deeper into their potential without them realising it.

Scientists have come to a consensus that the placebo effect is a self-fulfilling prophecy where the human brain decides upon an outcome and then works to ensure that the outcome is fulfilled. The placebo effect makes it clear that the mind is exceptionally powerful; numerous studies have concluded that real chemical changes take place in the brain just by thinking something is real even though it is fake. So just believing that you have another 60% left within you is enough to make it possible.

Since the placebo effect has proven to be true, it is possible to overcome the strongest addictions simply by changing one's attitude about that addiction. If a person expects to overcome an addiction, it's more likely that they will beat it as opposed to believing that they have no power over it. Regardless of the goal, you may have, you can improve your discipline levels by changing the way you think about the goal. The 40% rule and the placebo effect both let us know that we are capable of much more than we think, so whenever you find yourself making excuses not to do something or lacking discipline, put those principles into practice.

Take Control of Arousal: When we are in a highly stressful situation, large doses of adrenaline and cortisol are released, and the fight, flight or freeze response is activated, it is very difficult to override this process. Navy SEALs, on the other hand, have mastered the art of controlling these responses because, depending on the situation, their inability to do so can mean the difference between life or death. One of the techniques they use is called box breathing; when a SEAL starts to feel anxious and overwhelmed, they regain control by focusing on their breath. They breathe in for four seconds, hold their breath for four seconds, and breathe out for four seconds. This is repeated until the heart rate slows down.

A stressed-out mind is uncreative and inefficient, and so if you want to operate at your full potential, you must be capable of remaining calm. You can use box breathing anywhere at any time as soon as you start experiencing physical symptoms of stress. You will often hear experts advising people to manage stress; I don't agree, I believe it's better to stop it altogether than manage it.

Expand Your Vision and Get Better Results: Gary P. Latham and Edwin A. Locke, the pioneers of "A Theory of Goal Setting and Task Performance", state that setting difficult but realistic goals enhances our performance when it comes to pursuing that goal. Mediocre goals don't fill us with as much fire as challenging ones, and this results in putting the least amount of effort into achieving it. Let's say you have booked a trip to China, and you set a goal to learn some of the languages before you get there. Research suggests that setting your goals slightly higher, like learning how to speak the language at an intermediate level within a few months, are more likely to yield better results than just learning the basics. You may have to commit a lot more time into learning how to speak another language at an intermediate level. Still, it is more likely that you will be more disciplined and motivated to achieve a bigger goal.

The 10X Rule: Grant Cardone developed the 10X rule, which states that you should set goals that are ten times more than your original goal because it will make you take ten times more action towards it.

The 10X rule is purposely designed to force you to think about the way you view your possibilities and how you are going to go about accomplishing these targets.

Your thoughts and actions have created your current existence, and if you want to push past your barriers and get more out of life, you must first start thinking and acting in a way that far supersedes what you initially considered to be the norm. Let's use weight loss as an example if you set a goal to lose 5 pounds, apply the 10X rule, and plan to lose 50 pounds. Even though you don't need to lose 50 pounds, what it will do is put you in the mindset to change your diet and exercise habits for the long term as opposed to the few short weeks it will take to lose 5 pounds.

The 10X rule aims to maximise your potential; if you believe you are more capable than what you first thought, you will plan to achieve more, which in turn will enhance your discipline.

It's not uncommon for us to set low-grade goals for ourselves so that when we fail, we don't feel so bad, but if you are not willing to get more out of life, you will remain stuck at a mediocre level.

The 10 Minute Rule: Since the human brain is more developed than any other species, you would assume that we had better decision-making skills. But a Harvard University study has proved this not to be the case. During the research, chimpanzees and humans were both given the same choice, to get two treats straight away, or to get six treats in two minutes. The humans chose to wait 19% of the time while the chimpanzees chose to wait 72% of the time.

So, what happened here? Because I for one, refuse to believe that chimpanzees are smarter than humans.

The issue is that the human brain is overdeveloped, we overthink our decisions with obvious answers, and we are capable of rationalising bad behaviour which cheats us out of a more desirable outcome. Often, we can't tell the difference between an excuse and justification. This is where the 10 Minute Rule is effective if you are on a diet and you decide that you want a piece of cake, wait for 10 minutes before going to get it. This leaves no room for excuses or debates, if after the 10 minutes, you still feel like you want the piece of cake, you can either eat it or wait another 10 minutes to see if you still want it since you have already waited 10 minutes. By choosing to remain, you remove the "immediate" from immediate gratification and improve your decision-making skills and enhance your discipline.

The 10-minute rule also works in reverse; let's say you are running on the treadmill and you start to feel tired, keep pushing for another 10 minutes and see how you feel, after doing it once, you can do it again and again until you've truly pushed yourself to the limit.

As you know, there is nothing easy about being disciplined; even Navy SEALs are not born with discipline; they developed it over time by implementing strategies such as the 40% rule. They learned how to remain focused and calm in stressful situations, everyone is capable of living a more disciplined life, and the SEALs are evidence that it is possible.

What is Preventing You from Cultivating Positive Habits?

Energy vampires are people who suck the life out of you with their negative attitude, but did you know that there are also things that can drain you of your discipline?

Most people are well aware that they need the discipline to get what they want out of life, but why is it that so many of us are unable to apply the level of discipline required to reach our full potential? I don't believe in playing the blame game; everyone must take responsibility for their own life; however, there are some sly undercover ways that self-discipline can bypass you without you realising. Maybe the people you associate with are bad influences; you may have harmful habits or negative thought patterns that you are unaware of. You might hold the wrong belief system about discipline, or you might have the wrong motivations for what you are working towards.

The good news is that whatever it is, you can change it.

False Hope Syndrome: The False Hope Syndrome is the belief that changing your behavioural patterns is going to be easy. As a result, we set our expectations too high, which guarantees our failure. We completely underestimate how difficult it is to dismantle bad habits and imagine that we are going to land in our place of purpose without any bumps in the road. False hope leads to perpetual failure, which further solidifies the behaviour we want to change. Psychology professor Peter Herman states that people fail more than they succeed even though we have the best of motivations and intentions because we aim for extreme transformations that are unsustainable.

You might have a moment of clarity about colliding with destiny and how you are going to achieve it, but when life gets the better of you, that moment of clarity fades into obscurity, and your main focus is on getting through the day and not on achieving your life goals.

It takes time to achieve big goals; it's not an overnight process; every successful person you see plastered across the front covers of magazines and newspapers has a story of years of struggle behind them. The majority of people desire to be successful, but when reality sets in about the level of hard work it takes to get there, we put the idea to bed.

Outside of success, addiction is one of the biggest mountains to climb, for example, trying to quit smoking cold turkey is a recipe for disaster, people try and fail and get disappointed in themselves when they are unable to quit. The problem is that they fail to understand the extent of the physical and psychological addiction they are bound to. There is more to giving up smoking than simply making a decision, smokers have got to wean themselves off the addictive nicotine chemical, and this takes time. Instead, it would be more beneficial to set a goal to reduce the number of cigarettes smoked each month until complete abstinence has been achieved. The result is the same, you've quit smoking, but you have made it easier for yourself by breaking down those goals into more manageable, realistic milestones. Overcoming addiction in this way gives the brain time to carve out new neural pathways so that you can slowly change your habits.

So, what does your goal setting look like? Do they reflect what you are currently capable of, or are they based on the superhuman version of yourself that won't face any opposition? Avoiding false hope is essential to remaining disciplined when pursuing your goals. Being realistic about sustainability is very important when it comes to self-discipline and motivation because, ultimately, it will lead to a better outcome.

Discipline Versus Procrastination: Procrastination sabotages self-discipline because we justify our lack of action by waiting for the right conditions to get things done. For example, it's easy to take a day off from going to the gym because your arms are sore, that's just an excuse because you can work your legs or do cardio instead of working your arms. The only way to improve self-discipline is to stop waiting until you are ready or for you to feel like you are in the mood. Making excuses and inaction are cousins; there is no difference between the two; they both lead to the same destination – failure. When the conditions are just right, you've already lost because it means that you will never break out of your comfort zone.

If you are constantly making excuses now, nothing is stopping you from making them in the future. There is no such thing as the perfect circumstances; it doesn't exist; something is always going to be out of alignment. What appears to be logical procrastination is dangerous because it can apply to any circumstance. If you decide that you are going to stop smoking when work becomes less stressful, you will never quit because there is always going to be some level of stress at work. When you make the excuse that you are going to wait for circumstances to improve, you are telling yourself that you are incapable now, so if you are incapable now who says you are not going to be incapable in the future.

Anytime you step outside of your comfort zone, you are always going to have doubts. Challenges are attractive because they can be exciting, but the fear of them can also repel you. It's natural to doubt yourself when you are attempting something that you don't have the credentials for or when you are trying to overcome an obstacle. But whether it's starting a business, getting healthy, or writing a book, now is the best time to start. Spending days planning how you are going to reach your goal is another form of logical procrastination, the more time you spend planning and not doing increases your chances of never getting started in the first place. Get going and figure out the details as you move.

Society has also created an unhealthy belief system that everyone should be striving for perfection. This encourages procrastination because perfection is impossible to achieve, so we become afraid of failure and never start. You spur yourself into action when you recognise that the desire for perfection and procrastination are nothing but obstacles preventing you from becoming disciplined and successful.

One strategy to overcome procrastination and the temptation of perfection is the 75% rule, which states that you should take action when you are 75% certain that you will succeed. The reality is that you will never be 100% certain. You can't think yourself into discipline because it involves consistent action, and that's the only way you are going to master it. So, when you get to that 75% point, make a decision and commit to it. For example, you might want to run a marathon, but you know you are out of shape and could probably only run two miles if you're lucky. That's 75%, and that's where your training should begin. After a few weeks of training, you might start to feel that you could run half a marathon and with a few more months training, a full marathon. Again, this is the process of breaking down your larger goals into small actionable steps. As an ultra-distance runner once said - "I never ran a thousand miles. I could never do that. I ran one mile a thousand times."

Parkinson's Law: People who procrastinate often use the excuse that they work best under pressure, and there is a law to validate this justification. British historian Cyril Parkinson pioneered Parkinson's Law; it states that when we have a certain amount of time available, the work will expand to fill that time.

Parkinson became aware of the trend while he was a part of the British Civil Service. He noticed that as bureaucracies expanded, efficiency decreased, the more time and space people were given, the more of it they took. Parkinson found that menial tasks were made even more difficult to fill the allotted time. When there was a tight deadline, the task was simplified and completed faster.

One of the ways you can avoid failure is not to submit to Parkinson's Law; you can do this by setting yourself deadlines for your tasks. When you put a time limit on something, you force yourself to focus on the most important aspects of that task, and you won't complicate things to fill the extra time that you've got. In this way, you are challenging yourself consistently, and you'll avoid falling into the Parkinson's law trap. When you put the pressure on to finish early, you free your mind.

When you are trying to work out what's affecting your discipline, pay attention to your actions.

In what ways are you self-sabotaging? Discipline is difficult and unpleasant, but we also tend to make it harder on ourselves.

In 2003, Dave Brailsford was hired as the performance director for the British cycling team. They hadn't won a single event in 110 years; their reputation was so bad that top bike manufacturers in Europe refused to sell bikes to the team because they didn't want their failure to be associated with their brand!

Everything changed after Brailsford was hired, he implemented a strategy he named "the aggregation of marginal gains". The theory is that you search for tiny margins of improvement in everything you do, but when you put those things together, you have made a significant improvement. He applied the principle to cycling; he believed if there was at least a 1 percent improvement in everything related to bike riding, the team could turn things around.

Small Habits are the Fastest Way to Your Destination
Brailsford and his team started by making small changes, they applied alcohol to the tires to give them a better grip, they made the seats more comfortable, they changed their clothing to make them more aerodynamic, hundreds of minor changes were made, and as they accumulated, the team began to build momentum, and things began to change very quickly.

Within five years, the British Cycling team won an astonishing 60 percent of the gold medals at the 2008 Olympic Games in Beijing. Four years later, they set seven world records and nine Olympic records at the Olympic Games in London. Bradley Wiggins later became the first British cyclist to win the Tour de France. The following year his teammate Chris Froome took the title, and Wiggins won again for the next three years. During the years 2007 and 2017, there were so many victories that those nine years are regarded as the most successful period in cycling history.

What happened? How did a team go from being such failures that manufacturers would rather not sell them products for fear of ruining their reputation to becoming world champions?

I am certain that despite Brailsford's credentials, people were mocking him and telling him that he needed to train them harder, not change their clothing. But he knew what he was doing; he understood the science behind the accumulation of small changes.

One of the main reasons why people keep failing is because they assume that massive success requires massive action, and we overlook the small stuff. Whether its losing weight, writing a book, starting a business, or any other goal, we stress ourselves out, trying to make some ground-breaking improvements that will change the world, and it's not necessary.

Making a 1 percent improvement may not seem like a big deal, there is a chance that you won't even notice it, but you will appreciate it in the long run. Think about it, if you get 1 percent better at lifting weights each day, by the end of the year you will be 365 percent better!

As you repeat your habits, they multiply, you won't notice while you are doing them, but when you look back later down the line, you will see a big improvement in your life.

The same principle applies to bad habits; the person with lung cancer didn't get it after smoking their first cigarette, one turned into two, two turned into three, etc., and more and more damage was being done to their lungs as they continued to smoke.

This is a difficult concept to welcome into your life with open arms because we are not concerned with small changes; we want to see the big reveal. If you save $5 today you won't become a millionaire, if you go to the gym for one week, you won't see any abs, if you learn Spanish for 1 hour a night for a week you won't master the basics. What happens is that because we don't see immediate changes, we jump to the conclusion that it's not working and give up.

Making small changes to your daily routine will send your life into the direction that you desire.

Success is often misrepresented; we see the glitz and the glamour and assumed that it just happened for them. But what we are not aware of are the daily habits that went into becoming who they are now.

You reap what you sow. Your outcomes are the result of your habits. If you have no money in the bank, it's because you've got bad spending habits. If you are overweight, it's because you've got bad eating habits. If your house is untidy, it's because you've got lousy cleaning habits.

Now that you understand that your life is the result of your accumulated habits, you can predict where you are going to be in the next ten or twenty years if you continue down the path you are currently on. If you want to change, you must change your habits. Time will either work for you or against you, when people make the statement, "Time flies," what they're saying is they haven't achieved anything, they are in the same job they hate, living in the same run-down neighbourhood, dreaming the same dreams.

Some people are reading this book will skip right over this section to get to read about the habits of the rich, hoping that there will be a magic pill answer to their problems. But having knowledge of the habits are pointless if you don't understand how habits work and how to make them work for and not against you.

What Does Progress Look Like?

Imagine you are sitting in a room so cold that you can see your breath, there's a table in front of you with an ice cube on it, the temperature starts of at twenty-five degrees and then starts to heat up at 1-degree increments. The ice-cube is still hard at thirty-one degrees, but at thirty-two degrees, it starts to melt. It didn't take one degree for the ice to melt; the ice was melting all along; you just couldn't see it.

Every breakthrough moment is the result of a build-up of several previous actions.

In the same way, habits don't seem like they are making any difference until you can do something you couldn't do before. When you first start any challenge, you are going to feel disappointed in the beginning stages because you expect to make massive changes, but it feels as if the universe isn't rewarding you for your efforts. This is good news, as long as you are doing something, the fact that you are not going anywhere is a sign that you are going somewhere.

If you are finding it hard to build good habits, it's not because you are incapable, you just haven't hit that threshold yet. There is no point in getting upset or complaining that you've been running every day for a month and can't see a difference in your body; your only option is to continue. When you finally make that breakthrough, when the abs start forming, when the business takes off, those on the outside looking in are going to refer to it as an overnight success when you know it's taken hours of hard labour to get you there.

I refer to bad habits as sycamore trees, they are about 75 to 90 feet tall, and although their roots are shallow, they are 50 to 70 feet wide. Think about the amount of effort it will take to dig up such a tree! In other words, it takes time to uproot bad habits, you've probably been performing them for years, and you are not going to get rid of them overnight.

Educate Yourself: When you are aware of how your bad habit is harming your life, it will motivate you to change. Here is a funny story I heard from public speaker Les Brown. He had a friend who was severely overweight, everyone would tell him that he needs to lose some pounds, but he would always make the excuse that this is just the way he is, he is big-boned, and there is nothing he can do about it. He eventually got sick, and they had to call an ambulance, when he was taken to the hospital the doctor began to explain all the things that could happen to him if he did not lose weight one of them was that he could get diabetes and that could render him impotent. Everything else that he heard did not affect him, but as soon as he heard the word impotence, he made up his mind that he was going to change his life. Today this man is an entirely different person. He has dropped the pounds, he eats well, and he works out continuously.

What is your bad habit? Is it a bad diet? Do you spend too much time watching TV? Do you spend too much time asleep? Whatever bad habit you wish to overcome, take the time out to educate yourself on the negative consequences, and it will give you extra motivation to replace it with a good habit.

Reward Yourself: Experts suggest that we are motivated to behave in a certain way because of our desire for external rewards. One theory of human motivation is referred to as 'the incentive theory,' and it states that the desire for incentives or reinforcement motivates our behaviour. The theory argues that we are led away from actions that lead to negative consequences and pushed towards behaviours that lead to positive consequences. However, if that reward does not motivate us, we will not carry out the behavior.

Take time out to celebrate all your major milestones with your friends, family or team.

Enjoying each success not only rewards you, but magnifies the feeling of achievement and creates adds to the positive atmosphere around your project.

You know yourself better than anybody else, which means that you know what is going to motivate you to work towards your goals. The idea is to attach a reward to your goal, so if you have a bad habit of coming home from work taking off your shoes and having dinner while you sit in front of the TV and watch your favourite program, record the TV program, and then look forward to watching it after you have completed your goal. If you're struggling to think about a reward you can give yourself, here are some examples:

- Buy some concert tickets
- Visit your favourite art gallery
- Book tickets to the opera or theatre
- Have a glass of wine
- Take the family or your team out for a meal
- Get a manicure
- Buy a pair of shoes or clothes to reinforce your new self-image.
- Get to that spa you always wanted to visit.

The Way the Brain Works

The brain is made up of two hemispheres the left and the right; they are connected by what is called the corpus callosum. The right hemisphere is responsible for our imagination, and the left hemisphere is responsible for logic. The electrical signals that travel through this pathway communicate with every cell fibre and bone in our body to turn our thoughts into reality. This means that the simple act of thinking about your goals and dreams at the same time as writing them down activates the right and the left hemisphere, which encourages you to take action towards your goal.

How do You See Yourself?

The way you see yourself will determine your behaviour and your performance. Your level of self-esteem is crucial to your ability to succeed. Self-esteem is a simple concept, at a basic level; it means how much you like yourself. When you respect and like yourself, you believe you deserve the best out of life. The more confidence you have, the better you will perform at the task that you set for yourself. Self-esteem is the key to peak performance.

Your emotional health is also dependent upon your self-esteem. When you don't like yourself, that tiny voice deep within your soul is continually telling you that you're not good enough and diminishing your value. Self-esteem is the foundation for success; if you have got high self-esteem, you have a foundation to build on.

There are many reasons why people suffer from low self-esteem, but one of them is that they are not where they need to be in life. And if you want to go a little bit deeper, low self-esteem is the result of negative childhood experiences that you have carried with you into adulthood. The good news is that you can improve your self-esteem, and you can start by changing the way you see yourself.

In cognitive behavioural therapy, you learn about something called '**thought replacement**'; this is a simple concept that involves replacing negative thoughts with positive ones.

As we saw earlier, the way we speak to ourselves contributes to low self-esteem. One of the ways to combat this is to change the conversation that goes on in your head – to change how we see ourselves. If you see yourself as rich, powerful, deserving; if you value your time as a precious commodity; then you will start to act like that, subconsciously choosing rich habits over poor.

Many of our thoughts are unconscious. We are unaware of them. However, when you do catch yourself thinking negative thoughts change them. And you can do this with affirmations. Many successful people are staunch advocates of affirmations. Oprah Winfrey starts her mornings by speaking positive words over her life. You can make affirmation cards and carry them with you throughout the day. You can start your morning by speaking positive affirmations, and then when you're battling negative thoughts throughout the day; you can combat them by repeating affirmations. Here are some examples:

Negative Thought: *"I am never going to achieve anything in life."*
Affirmation: *"I am smart and intelligent enough to achieve everything that I want to accomplish."*

Negative Thought: *"I'm never going to have the money to do what I need to."*
Affirmation: *"I have everything I need to accomplish my goals."*

Negative thoughts: *"I don't deserve love."*
Affirmation: *"I am a beautiful person, and I deserve to be loved for who I am."*

Saying affirmations will feel uncomfortable at first because you are so used to hearing that negative voice. Positive affirmations also contradict your current circumstances, so you may look around and see poverty, yes, your bank account is empty, no you do not have a loving partner, yes you are slightly overweight; however, it is important to understand your circumstances do not define you, your situation is temporary. As you continue to speak these affirmations, the negative information that has been stored in your subconscious mind will be replaced with words of success and prosperity. You will then begin to attract the things that you want in your life.

How to Keep Yourself Motivated, Inspired, and Focused on Your Goal.

As we have already learned, motivation runs out; if you don't motivate yourself every day, you will struggle to achieve your goals.

Here are some tips to get you started:

Visualisation: a visualisation is a common tool used in personal development; it gives you a laser-sharp focus and motivates you to work towards your goal.

According to many of the world's top coaches, sport is 90% mental and 10% physical, the majority of people believe that it's the other way around.

Improved performance is one of the reasons why athletes dedicate so much of their time to visualisation. However, it is not as simple as it has been made out, it is a skill that you must practise in order to master there are four components to visualisation, realism, relaxation, reinforcement and regularity.

The Visualization Process: Find somewhere quiet and private where you will not be disturbed, focus on your breath and clear everything from your mind. Once you feel relaxed start thinking about what you want to achieve, keep taking deep breaths throughout this process. Visualise your success in as much detail as you can, add emotions and feelings to the vision so that you feel as if you have already achieved it.

Create a vision board: As well as being able to see what you want mentally; it is equally as important to be able to see what you want physically.

A vision board comes in handy for this. It involves getting some old magazines and newspapers and cutting out everything that resembles what you want. For example, if you desire to own a business, cut out a picture of a company; if you desire to own a Bentley, cut out a picture of a Bentley; if you want to get married, cut out a picture of two people walking down the aisle. I think you get my point; stick all these things on the vision board and place them somewhere where you will be able to see them every day.

You can also now download apps so that your vision board is readily available on your phone or your desktop. You can incorporate the vision board into your visualisation process by spending time looking at everything that you want to achieve before going into the time of meditation. When you can see what you want with your eyes, it is easier to visualise it in your mind and experience the accompanying emotions and feelings that accelerate the visualisation process.

Ok, so now you know all about visualisation it's also important to understand that you've got to take action.

Many of us have been led to believe that all we need to do is sit down, visualise and meditate, feel and believe and we will achieve our dreams. This is definitely not the case. When you listen to success stories, they will all say the same thing, they use the process of visualisation and a lot of the other law of attraction techniques, but they also took massive action. The purpose of visualization is to motivate you to do what you need to do to succeed.

Complete an Act of Power: The first lesson the people who protect our country learn when they join the military is how to make their bed. You would think that people training to protect America against things like terrorism would focus on something a bit more important. But it is not just an American principle, no matter what country you are in, when you join the military services your first lesson is in bed making, and I don't mean they just throw the covers over the bed and get on with their day. They learn and master how to make their beds. If there was such a thing as a bed making competition, the soldier would always get first prize.

What is the purpose of this? To protect them against gunfire on the battlefield? No, it won't, but what it does is instil a habit of excellence into the soldiers. As we have discussed, people operate according to their habits.

It is the small habits that count because they are an indicator of how you are going to do everything else in life. In other words, if a soldier cannot make his bed correctly, what business does he have defending his country? Can you imagine walking into an army barracks and seeing the place looking like a complete mess with clothes on the floor, bed unmade and dishes in the sink! What faith would you have in the military? None! Your first thought would be if they can't keep their own living space clean, how are they going to protect us when the enemy is attacking us?

Navy SEAL Admiral William McRaven gave a speech at the University of Texas, and he spoke about the most important lessons he has learned whilst being trained as a SEAL. He said that one of the only reasons why he is where he is today is because he was trained to make his bed every day. He went on to explain that even though making a bed is such a simple task, many people don't do it, and it sets the tone for the rest of the day.

The smallest task of making your bed is an achievement. If you're going to be successful, your day should be made up of a cluster of small achievements. Your aim is to do something small everyday day that will lead to you achieving your final dream. Making your bed provides momentum, and it encourages you to move onto the next task. You don't need to make your bed like a Navy SEAL, but what I'm saying is that if you are faithful in the small things, bigger things will begin to manifest in your life.

6. How to Stick with Your Habits Over Time

"Good habits are worth being fanatical about." John Irving

We all know the feeling of starting a good habit only to fall back into our bad habits a few days later. It appears that the habits that are good for us like exercise, journaling, and meditation are great for a day or two, and then they just become a burden. Bad habits almost seem to be a part of our DNA, and there doesn't seem to be an end in sight. No matter how hard you try, unhealthy habits like smoking, eating junk food, procrastinating, and watching too much television are impossible to overcome.

There are two reasons why changing our bad habits is challenging. First, we focus on changing the wrong thing, and second, we focus on changing them in the wrong way.

Let me break this down a bit further.

Change Has Got Layers
Change is like an onion, there are layers to it, and each one has its own unique set of issues:

Changing Your Outcomes: When you set a goal, you aim to change an outcome, you want to make a six or seven-figure sum, win the gold medal in your sport of choice, lose weight, etc.

Changing Your Process: The second level is about changing your systems and habits, developing a meditation practice, getting your desk organised, or getting to the gym every day. Habit building is associated with this level.

Changing Your Identity: If you are going to succeed at the first level, you must change your identity, and this involves changing your mindset - the way you think about yourself and others, your worldview, and your entire belief system.

Outcomes are about results; processes are about what you do. Your identity is rooted in your belief system; it's not difficult to work out what a person believes because it is reflected in their lifestyle. When it comes to building habits that last and developing a system of 1 percent improvement, the problem starts because of where we begin. When the focus is on what you want to achieve, you are not focusing on these changes becoming a lifestyle, you are focused on the outcome, and this isn't sustainable.

Think about two people who have decided to quit smoking, when offered a cigarette; one person states, *"I'll pass thanks, I'm trying to give up."* On the surface, this sounds like a really good response, but the problem is in their belief system, they still see themselves as someone who smokes but is trying to give up. Although they have a desire to change their behaviour, they still hold the same belief system. The second person responds with, *"No thanks, I don't smoke."* The wording is slightly different, but the second person has decided to change their identity, smoking is something they used to do, but the habit is no longer a part of their life.

The majority of people don't even contemplate changing their identity when they decide they want to make improvements in their life, they decide I want a body like Michael B Jordan (outcome), and if I stick to this gym routine and diet, I will get there (process).

People set goals without realising how their belief system drives their actions.

Behind every action is a belief system that drives the behaviour, and if the action does not line up with the belief system, it won't last. If you desire to have more money, but you are constantly spending instead of creating, you will always find that you are pulled in the direction of spending instead of earning. You may want to improve your health, but if you would rather relax on the sofa instead of work on reaching your health goals, you will remain stagnant. It is virtually impossible to change your habits if you don't change the belief system that led to the behaviour. When you get fired up about your new goals and your new plans without changing who you are, failure is inevitable.

Brian Clark is a very successful entrepreneur from Boulder, Colorado. Clark used to bite his nails constantly; it started as a nervous habit when he was a child but then changed into an unhealthy grooming ritual as he got older. One day, he decided that he was going to stop biting his nails until they had some length to them. With an immense amount of willpower, he was able to achieve this goal. He later asked his wife to book him a manicure appointment; he figured that if he were paying to maintain his nails, he would stop biting them. It worked, the manicure gave his hands an entirely different look, and he liked what he saw. The manicurist even told him that he would have healthy nails if he would stop biting them. He now had a new-found love for his nails; he was proud of them and wanted to keep them looking nice, so he stopped biting them. Even though he hadn't set out to stop biting his nails, the fact that he now liked his nails made all the difference.

When your habits become a part of your identity, that's when the change happens. If you take pride in your identity, you are going to care for it. If you take pride in the way your biceps look, you are going to want to keep them that way and the desire to keep them looking that way will outweigh your desire to turn the alarm off in the morning. If you take pride in the way your hair looks, you will develop rituals to ensure that your hair remains in good condition. Once you are proud of your identity, you will fight to maintain your habits.

The only way you are going to stick to good habits is if they become a part of your identity, motivation to achieve a specific goal is not enough. Anyone can convince themselves to stick to an exercise and diet regime to prepare for a cancer research marathon. A goal has been set, you put a system in place, but as soon as that goal has been achieved, you fall right back into your old habits because the new habits didn't become a part of who you are, they were only temporary.

- Your goal shouldn't be to read one book, but to become someone who is always reading.
- Your goal shouldn't be to run a marathon, but to become a runner.
- Your goal shouldn't be to make extra money to go on vacation, but to build wealth for generations.
- Your goal shouldn't be to learn how to play the piano, but to become a musician.

Your behaviour reflects your identity, whether consciously or unconsciously, what you do, speaks loudly about who you are.

Research suggests that once a person believes in a certain aspect of their identity, their behaviour will line up with that belief. You won't need to convince yourself to do certain things when it becomes a part of your identity because you are no longer trying to change your behaviour, you are simply acting in accordance with who you believe you are.

In the same way, your habits can work for or against you; your identity can do the same:

- I'm really bad at following directions
- I'm not good at math
- I'm not good with computers
- I'm never on time
- I always forget people's names
- I hate mornings

When you have spent your entire life rehearsing these narratives, you begin to accept them as facts, and you will resist any action that attempts to work against those narratives. Your subconscious mind is always going to fight to keep your behaviour in line with your belief system. It can feel comfortable to accept your cultural norms or continue to behave in a way that reflects your self-image even if it's not benefiting you. When you want to make positive changes in your life, but your identity conflicts with these changes, putting them into action becomes very difficult.

There are going to be days when your good habits take the back seat because you have other commitments, but this is rare because we can always find the time. On the days that you claim you are too busy; you will probably spend two or three hours scrolling through social media!

The real reason why you are unable to maintain good habits is that your identity is preventing you from doing so if you are going to make progress.

I believe that a set of laws governs the universe; if we live by them, we win, if we don't, we lose, it's as simple as that. If you want to change your behaviour, learn the appropriate laws, and apply them to your life.

That said, here are four laws that govern behaviour change.

1. **Expose Yourself to Your Cues:** Research psychologist and pioneer in the field of naturalistic decision making Gary Klein told the following story. A woman who had worked as a paramedic for several years went to a family gathering; when she got there and greeted her father in law, she told him that he didn't look right. He responded that he felt just fine and didn't feel that there was anything wrong. The former paramedic insisted that he went to hospital. He went, and it was discovered that one of his major arteries was blocked and he had to have a life-saving operation or he would have had a heart attack. If the daughter in law had not arrived when she did, there is a chance he could have died. What was it that the paramedic could see that evaded everyone else?

   When major arteries are blocked, the body copes by redirecting blood to the critical organs and away from peripheral locations near the surface of the skin. This causes an uneven distribution of blood to the face. Since the woman had spent several years working with people with heart failure, she was able to recognise the change in his face.

The same phenomenon is found in other fields such as the military; for example, military analysts tell the difference between the enemy fleet and their fleet even though the blip on the radar screen looks identical. An entire battleship was saved during the gulf war after Commander Michael Riley ordered to have a missile shot down even though it looked just like their battleships. He was right, but even his superiors were unable to understand how he did it.

Museum creators are capable of telling the difference between an authentic piece of artwork and an expertly designed counterfeit, although they are unable to tell you what it is about the counterfeit that made them realise it was a fake. Experienced radiologists can look at a brain scan and predict a stroke before there are any visible symptoms. It is even said that experienced hairdressers can tell when a woman is pregnant based on the texture of her hair.

The human brain is like a machine; it is constantly scanning the environment and analysing information. When you are always exposed to something, your brain will begin to store the most important and relevant information. With enough exposure to certain cues, you are capable of zoning in on those cues and predicting a certain outcome, although you haven't consciously thought about it. With experience, your brain will automatically begin to encode the lessons learned. We are not always capable of explaining what we are learning, but we are always learning, and your ability to tap into the relevant cues in your environment sets the stage for every habit that you have.

Our brain and our body perform the majority of its functions on autopilot, most of what we do is done without thinking. You do not tell your gut to digest, your hair to grow, your heart to beat, or your lungs to breathe, there is a lot more to you than you are consciously aware of. When you are hungry, you don't need to see the food to realise that you need to eat, the subconscious mind governs hunger and appetite. Several feedback loops within the body alert you when you need to eat and take note of what's going on within you and in your surroundings. Chemicals and hormones will let you know when you are hungry, although you are unaware of how this process takes place.

Therefore, when it comes to your habits, you don't need to be aware of the cue to indulge in the habit. When an opportunity arises, you take action without making a conscious decision to do so. This is why habits are so powerful and why they can work for or against you. Once you have developed a habit, your actions are no longer conscious, which is why people struggle to build good habits and break out of bad ones. The cues that drive our habits are invisible, and how we respond to them are deeply embedded within us. The urge to indulge in a habit will often come out of nowhere, which is why when it comes to changing our behaviour, we must start with awareness.

When you desire to develop a good habit, you must expose yourself to the cue attached to that habit. The more you see it; it will eventually become second nature to you to engage in the good habit. For example, if you want to start improving your spending habits, stick a reminder note on the mirror that you look in every morning, or change your phone screen to a reminder note so that you see it every time you look at your phone. This will remind you to stick to your budget, and you will start thinking twice every time you go to swipe your debit card.

2. **Make the Habit Irresistible:** Pay attention to your surroundings. What do you gravitate towards? Whatever you find attractive right? Whether it's food, the opposite sex, clothes, jewellery, etc., we have a burning desire for the things we are attracted to. Marketers take advantage of this and they spend millions distorting reality to get us hooked. Models are Photoshopped and edited to the point that their

own moms can no longer recognise them. The picture you see of the Bigmac displayed on billboards across the country looks nothing like the photographed image, but if you even get to the point of thinking about that it's too late, you've already pulled up at the drive-through and placed your order! Social media lavishes us with more praise in a few minutes than we can ever hope for at home or in the office. And let's not forget pornography, where videos are shot with the right combination of lighting and makeup to make footage that is irresistibly stimulating. Stimuli are so enticing that we can't control our instincts and we are driven to excessive shopping habits, porn habits, eating habits, social media habits and much more. If you want to increase the chances that a behaviour will occur, it must be attractive. While it might not be possible to turn every person into Brad Pitt or Rihanna, you can enhance their attractiveness.

Habits are driven by dopamine, also known as the feel-good hormone; it is what provides the gratifying sensation when we do something we like. Gambling, taking drugs, browsing social media, playing video games and eating junk food are all associated with higher levels of dopamine. However, dopamine is not only about pleasure. It plays a crucial role in several neurological processes such as memory, learning, motivation, voluntary movement, aversion and punishment. It is important to note that dopamine is also released when you anticipate pleasure. Heroin addicts experience an intense dopamine rush when they see a needle, not after they've shot up. Gambling addicts experience the same before they spin the wheel, not after a win. Whenever you anticipate that an opportunity will be rewarding, your dopamine levels increase and so does your motivation to experience the anticipated pleasure. Dopamine may explain why some men get so excited when they are chasing a woman, but after they have achieved their goal, they lose interest.

To make your habits more attractive, attach them to something you like. If you enjoy watching a show on Netflix, say to yourself that you will only watch the show when you are running on the treadmill. If you enjoy having a cup of coffee in the morning, say you will only have a cup of coffee once you have done 10 minutes of meditation or drunk a freshly squeezed fruit juice.

3. **Make it Easy:** Repetition is the key to mastering a habit. You don't need to perfect the habit, that will happen naturally over time, just practice it continuously. As you repeat an activity, you become more efficient because the structure of the brain changes to accommodate the activity. Neuroscientists refer to this as 'long-term potentiation,' which describes how the connection between neurons are strengthened based on the

activity that has taken place. The neuro connections strengthen with each repetition. All habits follow the same pattern, you start by making the effort to practice, and then it becomes automatic behaviour, a process known as automaticity. When you start performing a behaviour without thinking about it, you have reached automaticity. Repetition is how you make the habit easy.

4. **The Law of Least Effort:** The brain is wired to conserve as much energy as possible, it is human nature to take the path of least resistance. The law of least effort states that when two choices of varying difficulty are put before an individual, they will choose the easiest option. Humans are motivated to do what is easy. Everything we do requires energy, if it requires too much energy, we are less likely to do it. A goal of 50 squats per day takes a lot of energy. Initially, you are going to have the motivation to do it, but after a few days, you will lose the desire to keep putting that much effort into doing 50 squats and quit. On the other hand, it won't be too difficult to stick to doing one squat per day because it requires very little energy. The reason why bad habits such as watching television and scrolling through social media become so addictive is that they don't require any effort.

It is important to make your habits easy and convenient, so you are more likely to do them even when you don't feel like it. You can do this by practising environment design. **A great way to practice environment design is to make your cues more obvious.** When habits fit into the flow of your life, they are easier to develop. For example, if you want to improve your health by cooking more, arrange all your cooking utensils on the stove the night before so everything is readily available for you to make breakfast in the morning. If you want to exercise, put your gym clothes, shoes and water bottle out in the evening so that they are ready in the morning.

"The unexamined life is not worth living" Socrates.

Before we can build new habits, we must understand the old ones; I am not even going to pretend as if this process is easy, it's extremely difficult because we are unaware of them. However, you are one step ahead of the game; if you were not aware that you had bad habits that were negatively affecting your level of self-discipline, you wouldn't be reading this book. The fact that you know means that you have the power to change.

One of the most significant obstacles to changing bad habits is maintaining awareness of what we are doing. This is why the consequences of bad habits will often blindside us.

So, to start the process of getting rid of bad habits, I want you to create a "Habits Scorecard."

A Habits Scorecard

This is a simple exercise; it involves writing down everything you know you do every day. Here is an example:

- Wake up
- Switch off my alarm
- Go to the bathroom
- Brush my teeth
- Make a cup of coffee
- Check my phone
- Make my bed
- Take a shower
- Put makeup on
- Get dressed for work

Your list will be longer than this, make sure you write everything down no matter how irrelevant you think it is. Once you have done that, write next to each habit, whether it's good, bad, or neutral.

Whether a habit is good or bad will depend on what you are trying to achieve, for a person trying to lose weight, making a fried egg sandwich every morning will be considered a bad habit, but for someone who wants to build muscle, eating three boiled eggs every morning would be a good habit.

If you are finding it difficult to rate your habits, ask yourself whether it is benefiting you and if it is helping you to become your ideal person. For example, you might think that waking up at 7 am is a good habit, but you are trying to lose weight and don't have time to fit in a workout. A viable solution to this would be to wake up earlier so that you can fit in a workout; therefore, you would make waking up at 7 am as a bad habit.

A habits scorecard aims to get you to become aware of your habits. To ensure that it is accurate, if you have a partner, ask them to go over your list and check whether you haven't missed anything out. When you look at your scorecard, don't judge yourself, even if its praise for doing the right thing, if you eat a doughnut every morning, don't criticise yourself for not having any self-control. Instead, observe your habits as an outsider looking in.

Your journey to changing your habits has now begun, and you can start by calling yourself out. If you want to start a business and you have a bad habit of sitting in front of the TV every evening, say "I am going to watch TV, but if I do, I won't get this business started, and I won't have the money I need to send my kids to college." When your bad habits are spoken out loud, it brings them to the conscious mind, and you are now able to pay attention to the consequences of your actions as opposed to blindly slipping back into old habits.

Changing your behaviour always starts with awareness. An alcoholic or drug addict will never overcome their addiction if they don't acknowledge it. The same principle applies to the bad habits you have formed that are making it difficult for you to become self-disciplined and start building wealth.

How Long Does it Take to Develop a Habit?

You will often hear people say that it takes 21 days to create a habit; this isn't entirely true. In the 1950s, pioneering plastic surgeon Dr Maxwell Maltz started to notice an interesting pattern with his patients. After an operation, he found that it would take his patients 21 days to get used to their new face. Maltz also found that when a patient had a leg or an arm amputated, they would feel as if the limb was still a part of them for 21 days. These findings encouraged him to see how long it would take him to adjust to new behaviours, and he discovered that it also took him 21 days. What Dr Maltz stated was that it takes a minimum of 21 days for a new mental image to push out the old one. He later wrote his findings in his best-selling book called Psycho-Cybernetics, to date it has sold over 30 million copies.

In the decades that followed, the book has influenced almost every major self-help professional from Tonny Robbins to Zig Ziglar to Brian Tracy. And as more and more people began to speak about the contents of the book Psycho-Cybernetics, the facts started to change. This is how it came about that it takes 21 days to form a habit. It makes logical sense as to why 21 days became so popular, the time frame isn't too intimidating. It's not too short so that it's unbelievable, and neither is it too long so that its unattainable, twenty-one days makes people feel comfortable. But the problem is that this isn't what Dr Maltz discovered. He made it crystal clear that **it takes a MINIMUM of 21 days to adapt to change**. So how long does it take to form a habit?

How Long Does it Take to Form a Habit?

In a study published in the European Journal of Social Psychology, health psychologist Phillipa Lally analysed the habits of 96 participants over 12 weeks.

They all chose one new habit, and each day reported whether they performed the habit and how natural the behaviour felt. Some of the participants chose a simple habit, such as "finishing a bottle of water with lunch," while others chose harder tasks such as "jogging for 15 minutes before dinner." The researchers examined the reports to determine the length of time it took for the behaviour to become automatic.

The study concluded that on average, it takes 66 days for a new behaviour to become automatic. It is also important to mention that this number can vary depending on the circumstances, the person, and the behaviour. What Lally eventually found was that it took between 18 to 254 days to form a new habit. Another interesting finding was that missing a day or two during the habit-forming process does not erase the work that has already been done; you can pick up from where you left off.

The motivation for the Journey

Most of you have locked eyes on those 254 days and thought to yourself. "That's way too long; I'm never going to make it."

Well, if you look at it the right way, its good news. First, think about how you'd feel if you completed 21 days, and you still didn't feel that it had become second nature? You'd give up and probably never try again, assuming that this habit thing isn't for you. Lally's research gives us permission to enjoy the process and embrace the long, slow journey to greatness. Second, it lets us know that we don't need to be perfect; you can miss a day or two and still pick up where you left off. You shouldn't look at failure as the end but as a learning experience. What was it that caused you to miss a day, did you reach over and hit the snooze button? Put the alarm clock in another room so that when it goes off, you are forced to get out of bed and turn it off. Once you get up, you are far more likely to get on with what you need to do since you are already out of bed.

Finally, even though habit-forming may take some time, it teaches us that it's not an event that just magically happens but a process. The 21-day hype is dangerous; it gives people false hope that they can perform an action for three weeks and master it within that time without understanding that it is a system they must dedicate themselves to. Now that you understand this, you are at an advantage; you can now manage your expectations and commit to making small changes instead of pressuring yourself into thinking you've got to do it all at once.

What's Next

Whether it takes 21 days or 254, the length of time it takes to adopt a wealthy habit doesn't matter because there is no escape from the work you will need to put in. There is no shortcut to day 254, you've got to start from day one, so don't focus on numbers, focus on putting the work in.

Conclusion

"If you are going to achieve excellence in big things, you develop the habit in little matters." Colin Powell

Congratulations, you have come to the end of this book; this means you are not ordinary; neither are you average. You are truly exceptional! How do I know this? Because you have done something that the majority of people never do, you have started and finished reading a book! You have gone the extra mile. To establish habits that will take you to greater heights and breed success. It takes discipline to be persistent and stick to something, and the fact that you have read this book is a clear demonstration that you have what it takes to be successful.

Your Next step is to take action, have a meeting with yourself, and decide that you are going to start this journey. Stop where you are, start small and commit to doing at least one of these habits every day for five minutes. It may sound small, but those five minutes per day add up to more than 12 hours per month!

Everything starts with the decision. Where you are today is the result of a series of decisions that you have made, if you want to change your future, you must start making better decisions and you can do this by taking responsibility for the state of your life right now whether it's your mindset, your lifestyle, your relationships, or your finances, it is your responsibility to make the changes necessary to improve.

"There's only one person responsible for the quality of your life, and that person is you. Everything about you is a result of your doing or not doing. Your income. Your debt. Your relationships. Your health. Your fitness levels. Your attitude and behaviour. Everything. That person you see when you look in the mirror is the chief architect of your life." Jack Cranfield

Practising self-discipline is a lifestyle; it is not something that you do just to achieve a goal. It is something that you practice when nobody is watching; When you see successful people in the public eye, they have spent many years making private sacrifices. What you do behind closed doors is more important than what you do in public. During one of John Maxwell's lectures, a university graduate asked, *"John, I think your leadership principles are very powerful, but I don't have anybody to lead. Where can I start?"* Maxwell replied, *"That is an excellent question; start with you."* If you're going to lead other people, you must be able to lead yourself; you cannot pull anyone up the ladder if you can't get yourself up there.

If you are ashamed of your daily habits you know that you are in the wrong place, a great way to determine this is to ask yourself what would you do if a teenager asked to shadow you and copy your habits for five days. What will they learn from your rituals, routines and habits in your daily life? Would it motivate them to want to become more like you? What if they witness you getting up early, meditating, praying, and reading educational material? And then at 8 o'clock you state okay now let's get to work. This is going to inspire and motivate them to want to become more like you.

On the other hand, if your habits involve hitting the snooze button any time it goes off, rolling out of bed an hour before you've got to start work rushing around the house looking for documents and car keys. Stopping off at the drive-through to grab breakfast, do you think that teenager is going to be inspired to live your life? The simple answer to this question is no!

Do not despise small beginnings; it is difficult to continue working towards your goals when you're so far from them. However, when you understand that there is not one successful person who wrote down their dreams one day and was living them the next. They took action every day to achieve their dreams, often for many years. As you keep repeating good habits, they will soon become second nature, and you will begin to operate on autopilot.

The key to success is persistence. Remember, some of you spent the majority of your life living from a place of lack, your habits so far have shaped your conditions. It is going to take a while for you to undo the damage that has been done. Therefore, do not be too hard on yourself; when you fail, pick yourself up, brush yourself off, and start again. Do not entertain negative thoughts, that little voice within is going to try and convince you that there is no point in trying this; you are who you are; you will never reach your goals. At this point, pull out your affirmation cards and remind your voice that you are in a new person, and you are going to achieve everything that you have set out to!

Finally, I would like to stress that your impact on the world is measured by more than the size of your investment portfolio. Yes, your life is a miracle, but wouldn't it be even more satisfying if your life was a miracle for somebody else. Success extends beyond you and your family; once you arrive at your place of purpose, you are going to have the tools to inspire and motivate others. You will have the resources to help those less fortunate than yourself. I think about life like this; there are many people who are motivated me to get to where I am today. I spent a lot of time reading books, listening to motivational speakers, and going to seminars to boost my knowledge and give me the skills I needed to achieve my dreams. If those people who gave me access to the knowledge I needed had given up when things were not working out the way they had planned, there is a possibility that I would still be working a 9-to-5 today, just existing, going to work coming home and living a life without meaning.

I believe that we are all put on earth for a purpose, there is something that you were created to do that only you can do, and if you don't do it, it will get left on done. Life is about service to others; however, to do this with excellence, you must have arrived at a place where you are confident that you have enough resources within you to share with the world.

Your habits will determine how far you go in life, my question to you is how far do you want to go?

I wish you every success on your journey to building better habits and creating the life that you deserve!

Resources

Becraft, M. B. (2014). *Bill Gates: A Biography*. California, USA: Greenwood, An Imprint Of ABC-CLIO, LLC.

Burchard, B. (2017). *High-Performance Habits: How Extraordinary People Become That Way*. USA: Hay House, Incorporated.

Duhigg, C. (2013). *The Power of Habit: Why We Do what We Do and how to Change*. USA: Random House.

Covey, S. R. (2004). *The 7 Habits of Highly Effective People: Powerful Lessons in Personal Change*. New York, USA,: Free Press.

Tolle, E. (2001). *The Power of Now: A Guide to Spiritual Enlightenment*. USA: Hodder and Stoughton.

Graziosi, D. (2019). *Millionaire Success Habits: The Gateway to Wealth & Prosperity*. New York, USA: Hay House, Incorporated.

Huffington, A. S. (2014). *Thrive: The Third Metric to Redefining Success and Creating a Happier Life*. Croydon, United Kingdom: WH Allen.

Isaacson, W., Jobs, S., & Simon & Schuster. (2011). *Steve Jobs*. New York, USA: Simon & Schuster.

Ray, G. (2018). *Self Discipline: A How-To Guide to Stop Procrastination and Achieve Your Goals in 10 Steps Including 10 Day Bonus Online Coaching Course to Master Self-Discipline and Build Daily Goal-Crushing Habits*. USA: Amazon Digital Services LLC - Kdp Print Us.

Winfrey, O. (2019). *The Path Made Clear: Discovering Your Life's Direction and Purpose*. USA: Pan Macmillan.

BBC. *The Law that explains why you can't get anything done*.

About the author

Dan Keller is a self-help specialist, completely obsessed with anything that can improve his life and that of those around him.

At 30, Dan broke out of the rat race, quitting his 9-5 desk job in UK banking, to follow his dreams: living in a stunning place with financial independence. Now, as an author and entrepreneur, he lives an abundant life with his wife and two children that has exceeded his wildest expectations.

Everything that he has achieved in life came through applying the techniques shares in his books.

Dan was brought up in Yorkshire, England on the edge of the Peak District. When not writing, he loves to get out into nature and explore his adopted home, the French Riviera. He is a keen adventurer who enjoys photography, mountaineering, skiing, surfing and free diving.

Leave a review

As an independent author with a small marketing budget, reviews are my livelihood on this platform. If you enjoyed this book, I'd really appreciate it if you leave your honest feedback. You can do so on Amazon. I love hearing from my readers, and I personally read every review.

Thank you, Dan Keller.

Made in the USA
San Bernardino, CA
24 April 2020

69488427R00088